6. Enter your class ID code to join a class.

IF YOU HAVE A CLASS CODE FROM YOUR TEACHER

a. Enter your class code and click | Next |

b. Once you have joined a class, you will be able to use the Discussion Board and Email tools.

c. To enter this code later, choose **Join a Class**.

IF YOU DO NOT HAVE A CLASS CODE

a. If you do not have a class ID code, click | Skip |

b. You do not need a class ID code to use *iQ Online*.

c. To enter this code later, choose **Join a Class**.

7. Review registration information and click Log In. Then choose your book. Click **Activities** to begin using *iQ Online*.

IMPORTANT

- After you register, the next time you want to use *iQ Online*, go to www.iQOnlinePractice.com and log in with your email address and password.
- The online content can be used for 12 months from the date you register.
- For help, please contact customer service: eltsupport@oup.com.

WHAT IS iQ ONLINE?

All new activities provide essential skills **practice** and support.

Vocabulary and Grammar **games** immerse you in the language and provide even more practice.

Authentic, engaging **videos** generate new ideas and opinions on the Unit Question.

Go to the Media Center to download or stream all **student book audio**.

Use the **Discussion Board** to discuss the Unit Question and more.

Email encourages communication with your teacher and classmates.

Automatic grading gives immediate feedback and tracks progress.

Progress Reports show what you have mastered and where you still need more practice.

SHAPING learning TOGETHER

We would like to acknowledge the teachers from all over the world who participated in the development process and review of the Q series.

Special thanks to our Q: Skills for Success Second Edition Topic Advisory Board

Shaker Ali Al-Mohammad, Buraimi University College, Oman; **Dr. Asmaa A. Ebrahim**, University of Sharjah, U.A.E.; **Rachel Batchilder**, College of the North Atlantic, Qatar; **Anil Bayir**, Izmir University, Turkey; **Flora Mcvay Bozkurt**, Maltepe University, Turkey; **Paul Bradley**, University of the Thai Chamber of Commerce Bangkok, Thailand; **Joan Birrell-Bertrand**, University of Manitoba, MB, Canada; **Karen E. Caldwell**, Zayed University, U.A.E.; **Nicole Hammond Carrasquel**, University of Central Florida, FL, U.S.; **Kevin Countryman**, Seneca College of Applied Arts & Technology, ON, Canada; **Julie Crocker**, Arcadia University, NS, Canada; **Marc L. Cummings**, Jefferson Community and Technical College, KY, U.S.; **Rachel DeSanto**, Hillsborough Community College Dale Mabry Campus, FL, U.S.; **Nilüfer Ertürkmen**, Ege University, Turkey; **Sue Fine**, Ras Al Khaimah Women's College (HCT), U.A.E.; **Amina Al Hashami**, Nizwa College of Applied Sciences, Oman; **Stephan Johnson**, Nagoya Shoka Daigaku, Japan; **Sean Kim**, Avalon, South Korea; **Gregory King**, Chubu Daigaku, Japan; **Seran Küçük**, Maltepe University, Turkey; **Jonee De Leon**, VUS, Vietnam; **Carol Lowther**, Palomar College, CA, U.S.; **Erin Harris-MacLead**, St. Mary's University, NS, Canada; **Angela Nagy**, Maltepe University, Turkey; **Huynh Thi Ai Nguyen**, Vietnam; **Daniel L. Paller**, Kinjo Gakuin University, Japan; **Jangyo Parsons**, Kookmin University, South Korea; **Laila Al Qadhi**, Kuwait University, Kuwait; **Josh Rosenberger**, English Language Institute University of Montana, MT, U.S.; **Nancy Schoenfeld**, Kuwait University, Kuwait; **Jenay Seymour**, Hongik University, South Korea; **Moon-young Son**, South Korea; **Matthew Taylor**, Kinjo Gakuin Daigaku, Japan; **Burcu Tezcan-Unal**, Zayed University, U.A.E.; **Troy Tucker**, Edison State College-Lee Campus, FL, U.S.; **Kris Vicca**, Feng Chia University, Taichung; **Jisook Woo**, Incheon University, South Korea; **Dunya Yenidunya**, Ege University, Turkey

UNITED STATES **Marcarena Aguilar**, North Harris College, TX; **Rebecca Andrade**, California State University North Ridge, CA; **Lesley Andrews**, Boston University, MA; **Deborah Anholt**, Lewis and Clark College, OR; **Robert Anzelde**, Oakton Community College, IL; **Arlys Arnold**, University of Minnesota, MN; **Marcia Arthur**, Renton Technical College, WA; **Renee Ashmeade**, Passaic County Community College, NJ; **Anne Bachmann**, Clackamas Community College, OR; **Lida Baker**, UCLA, CA; **Ron Balsamo**, Santa Rosa Junior College, CA; **Lori Barkley**, Portland State University, OR; **Eileen Barlow**, SUNY Albany, NY; **Sue Bartch**, Cuyahoga Community College, OH; **Lora Bates**, Oakton High School, VA; **Barbara Batra**, Nassau County Community College, NY; **Nancy Baum**, University of Texas at Arlington, TX; **Rebecca Beck**, Irvine Valley College, CA; **Linda Berendsen**, Oakton Community College, IL; **Jennifer Binckes Lee**, Howard Community College, MD; **Grace Bishop**, Houston Community College, TX; **Jean W. Bodman**, Union County College, NJ; **Virginia Bouchard**, George Mason University, VA; **Kimberley Briesch Sumner**, University of Southern California, CA; **Kevin Brown**, University of California, Irvine, CA; **Laura Brown**, Glendale Community College, CA; **Britta Burton**, Mission College, CA; **Allison L. Callahan**, Harold Washington College, IL; **Gabriela Cambiasso**, Harold Washington College, IL; **Jackie Campbell**, Capistrano Unified School District, CA; **Adele C. Camus**, George Mason University, VA; **Laura Chason**, Savannah College, GA; **Kerry Linder Catana**, Language Studies International, NY; **An Cheng**, Oklahoma State University, OK; **Carole Collins**, North Hampton Community College, PA; **Betty R. Compton**, Intercultural Communications College, HI; **Pamela Couch**, Boston University, MA; **Fernanda Crowe**, Intrax International Institute, CA; **Vicki Curtis**, Santa Cruz, CA; **Margo Czinski**, Washtenaw Community College, MI; **David Dahnke**, Lone Star College, TX; **Gillian M. Dale**, CA; **L. Dalgish**, Concordia College, MN; **Christopher Davis**, John Jay College, NY; **Sherry Davis**, Irvine University, CA; **Natalia de Cuba**, Nassau County Community College, NY; **Sonia Delgadillo**, Sierra College, CA; **Esmeralda Diriye**, Cypress College & Cal Poly, CA; **Marta O. Dmytrenko-Ahrabian**, Wayne State University, MI; **Javier Dominguez**, Central High School, SC; **Jo Ellen Downey-Greer**, Lansing Community College, MI; **Jennifer Duclos**, Boston University, MA; **Yvonne Duncan**, City College of San Francisco, CA; **Paul Dydman**, USC Language Academy, CA; **Anna Eddy**, University of Michigan-Flint, MI; **Zohan El-Gamal**, Glendale Community College, CA; **Jennie Farnell**, University of Connecticut, CT; **Susan Fedors**, Howard Community College, MD; **Valerie Fiechter**, Mission College, CA; **Ashley Fifer**, Nassau County Community College, NY; **Matthew Florence**, Intrax International Institute, CA; **Kathleen Flynn**, Glendale College, CA; **Elizabeth Fonsea**, Nassau County Community College, NY; **Eve Fonseca**, St. Louis Community College, MO; **Elizabeth Foss**, Washtenaw Community College, MI; **Duff C. Galda**, Pima Community College, AZ; **Christiane Galvani**, Houston Community College, TX; **Gretchen Gerber**, Howard Community College, MD; **Ray Gonzalez**, Montgomery College, MD; **Janet Goodwin**, University of California, Los Angeles, CA; **Alyona Gorokhova**, Grossmont College, CA; **John Graney**, Santa Fe College, FL; **Kathleen Green**, Central High School, AZ; **Nancy Hamadou**, Pima Community College-West Campus, AZ; **Webb Hamilton**, De Anza College, San Jose City College, CA; **Janet Harclerode**, Santa Monica Community College, CA; **Sandra Hartmann**, Language and Culture Center, TX; **Kathy Haven**, Mission College, CA; **Roberta Hendrick**, Cuyahoga Community College, OH; **Ginny Heringer**, Pasadena City College, CA; **Adam Henricksen**, University of Maryland, MD; **Carolyn Ho**, Lone Star College-CyFair, TX; **Peter Hoffman**, LaGuardia Community College, NY; **Linda Holden**, College of Lake County, IL; **Jana Holt**, Lake Washington Technical College, WA; **Antonio Iccarino**, Boston University, MA; **Gail Ibele**, University of Wisconsin, WI; **Nina Ito**, American Language Institute, CSU Long Beach, CA; **Linda Jensen**, UCLA, CA; **Lisa Jurkowitz**, Pima Community College, CA; **Mandy Kama**, Georgetown University, Washington, DC; **Stephanie Kasuboski**, Cuyahoga Community College, OH; **Chigusa Katoku**, Mission College, CA; **Sandra Kawamura**, Sacramento City College, CA; **Gail Kellersberger**, University of Houston-Downtown, TX; **Jane Kelly**, Durham Technical Community College, NC; **Maryanne Kildare**, Nassau County Community College, NY; **Julie Park Kim**, George Mason University, VA; **Kindra Kinyon**, Los Angeles Trade-Technical College, CA; **Matt Kline**, El Camino College, CA; **Lisa Kovacs-Morgan**, University of California, San Diego, CA; **Claudia Kupiec**, DePaul University, IL; **Renee La Rue**, Lone Star College-Montgomery, TX; **Janet Langon**, Glendale College, CA; **Lawrence Lawson**, Palomar College, CA; **Rachele Lawton**, The Community College of Baltimore County, MD; **Alice Lee**, Richland College, TX; **Esther S. Lee**, CSUF & Mt. SAC, CA; **Cherie Lenz-Hackett**, University of Washington, WA; **Joy Leventhal**, Cuyahoga Community College, OH; **Alice Lin**, UCI Extension, CA; **Monica Lopez**, Cerritos College, CA; **Dustin Lovell**, FLS International Marymount College, CA; **Carol Lowther**, Palomar College, CA; **Candace Lynch-Thompson**, North Orange County Community College District, CA; **Thi Thi Ma**, City College of San Francisco, CA; **Steve Mac Isaac**, USC Long Academy, CA; **Denise Maduli-Williams**, City College of San Francisco, CA; **Eileen Mahoney**, Camelback High School, AZ; **Naomi Mardock**, MCC-Omaha, NE; **Brigitte Maronde**, Harold Washington College, IL; **Marilyn Marquis**, Laposita College CA; **Doris Martin**, Glendale Community College; Pasadena City College, CA; **Keith Maurice**, University of Texas at Arlington, TX; **Nancy Mayer**, University of Missouri-St. Louis, MO; **Aziah McNamara**, Kansas State University, KS; **Billie McQuillan**, Education Heights, MN; **Karen Merritt**, Glendale Union High School District, AZ; **Holly Milkowart**, Johnson County Community College, KS; **Eric Moyer**, Intrax International Institute, CA; **Gino Muzzatti**, Santa Rosa Junior College, CA; **Sandra Navarro**, Glendale Community College, CA; **Than Nyeinkhin**, ELAC, PCC, CA; **William Nedrow**, Triton College, IL; **Eric Nelson**, University of Minnesota, MN; **Than Nyeinkhin**, ELAC, PCC, CA; **Fernanda Ortiz**, Center for English as a Second Language at the University of Arizona, AZ; **Rhony Ory**, Ygnacio Valley High School, CA; **Paul Parent**, Montgomery College, MD; **Dr. Sumeeta Patnaik**, Marshall University, WV; **Oscar Pedroso**, Miami Dade College, FL; **Robin Persiani**, Sierra College, CA; **Patricia Prenz-Belkin**, Hostos Community College, NY; **Suzanne Powell**, University of Louisville, KY; **Jim Ranalli**, Iowa State University, IA; **Toni R. Randall**, Santa Monica College, CA; **Vidya Rangachari**, Mission College, CA; **Elizabeth Rasmussen**, Northern Virginia Community College, VA; **Lara Ravitch**, Truman College, IL;

ii

Deborah Repasz, San Jacinto College, TX; Marisa Recinos, English Language Center, Brigham Young University, UT; Andrey Reznikov, Black Hills State University, SD; Alison Rice, Hunter College, NY; Jennifer Robles, Ventura Unified School District, CA; Priscilla Rocha, Clark County School District, NV; Dzidra Rodins, DePaul University, IL; Maria Rodriguez, Central High School, AZ; Josh Rosenberger, English Language Institute University of Montana, MT; Alice Rosso, Bucks County Community College, PA; Rita Rozzi, Xavier University, OH; Maria Ruiz, Victor Valley College, CA; Kimberly Russell, Clark College, WA; Stacy Sabraw, Michigan State University, MI; Irene Sakk, Northwestern University, IL; Deborah Sandstrom, University of Illinois at Chicago, IL; Jenni Santamaria, ABC Adult, CA; Shaeley Santiago, Ames High School, IA; Peg Sarosy, San Francisco State University, CA; Alice Savage, North Harris College, TX; Donna Schaeffer, University of Washington, WA; Karen Marsh Schaeffer, University of Utah, UT; Carol Schinger, Northern Virginia Community College, VA; Robert Scott, Kansas State University, KS; Suell Scott, Sheridan Technical Center, FL; Shira Seaman, Global English Academy, NY; Richard Seltzer, Glendale Community College, CA; Harlan Sexton, CUNY Queensborough Community College, NY; Kathy Sherak, San Francisco State University, CA; German Silva, Miami Dade College, FL; Ray Smith, Maryland English Institute, University of Maryland, MD; Shira Smith, NICE Program University of Hawaii, HI; Tara Smith, Felician College, NJ; Monica Snow, California State University, Fullerton, CA; Elaine Soffer, Nassau County Community College, NY; Andrea Spector, Santa Monica Community College, CA; Jacqueline Sport, LBWCC Luverne Center, AL; Karen Stanely, Central Piedmont Community College, NC; Susan Stern, Irvine Valley College, CA; Ayse Stromsdorfer, Soldan I.S.H.S., MO; Yilin Sun, South Seattle Community College, WA; Thomas Swietlik, Intrax International Institute, IL; Nicholas Taggert, University of Dayton, OH; Judith Tanka, UCLA Extension–American Language Center, CA; Amy Taylor, The University of Alabama Tuscaloosa, AL; Andrea Taylor, San Francisco State, CA; Priscilla Taylor, University of Southern California, CA; Ilene Teixeira, Fairfax County Public Schools, VA; Shirl H. Terrell, Collin College, TX; Marya Teutsch-Dwyer, St. Cloud State University, MN; Stephen Thergesen, ELS Language Centers, CO; Christine Tierney, Houston Community College, TX; Arlene Turini, North Moore High School, NC; Cara Tuzzolino, Nassau County Community College, NY; Suzanne Van Der Valk, Iowa State University, IA; Nathan D. Vasarhely, Ygnacio Valley High School, CA; Naomi S. Verratti, Howard Community College, MD; Hollyhana Vettori, Santa Rosa Junior College, CA; Julie Vorholt, Lewis & Clark College, OR; Danielle Wagner, FLS International Marymount College, CA; Lynn Walker, Coastline College, CA; Laura Walsh, City College of San Francisco, CA; Andrew J. Watson, The English Bakery; Donald Weasenforth, Collin College, TX; Juliane Widner, Sheepshead Bay High School, NY; Lynne Wilkins, Mills College, CA; Pamela Williams, Ventura College, CA; Jeff Wilson, Irvine Valley College, CA; James Wilson, Consomnes River College, CA; Katie Windahl, Cuyahoga Community College, OH; Dolores "Lorrie" Winter, California State University at Fullerton, CA; Jody Yamamoto, Kapi'olani Community College, HI; Ellen L. Yaniv, Boston University, MA; Norman Yoshida, Lewis & Clark College, OR; Joanna Zadra, American River College, CA; Florence Zysman, Santiago Canyon College, CA;

CANADA Patricia Birch, Brandon University, MB; Jolanta Caputa, College of New Caledonia, BC; Katherine Coburn, UBC's ELI, BC; Erin Harris-Macleod, St. Mary's University, NS; Tami Moffatt, English Language Institute, BC; Jim Papple, Brock University, ON; Robin Peace, Confederation College, BC;

ASIA Rabiatu Abubakar, Eton Language Centre, Malaysia; Wiwik Andreani, Bina Nusantara University, Indonesia; Frank Bailey, Baiko Gakuin University, Japan; Mike Baker, Kosei Junior High School, Japan; Leonard Barrow, Kanto Junior College, Japan; Herman Bartelen, Japan; Siren Betty, Fooyin University, Kaohsiung; Thomas E. Bieri, Nagoya College, Japan; Natalie Brezden, Global English House, Japan; MK Brooks, Mukogawa Women's University, Japan; Truong Ngoc Buu, The Youth Language School, Vietnam; Charles Cabell, Toyo University, Japan; Fred Carruth, Matsumoto University, Japan; Frances Causer, Seijo University, Japan; Jeffrey Chalk, SNU, South Korea; Deborah Chang, Wenzao Ursuline College of Languages, Kaohsiung; David Chatham, Ritsumeikan University, Japan; Andrew Chih Hong Chen, National Sun Yat-sen University, Kaohsiung; Christina Chen, Yu-Tsai Bilingual Elementary School, Taipei; Hui-chen Chen, Shi-Lin High School of Commerce, Taipei; Seungmoon Choe, K2M Language Institute, South Korea; Jason Jeffree Cole, Coto College, Japan; Le Minh Cong, Vungtau Tourism Vocational College, Vietnam; Todd Cooper, Toyama National College of Technology, Japan; Marie Cosgrove, Daito Bunka University, Japan; Randall Cotten, Gifu City Women's College, Japan; Tony Cripps, Ritsumeikan University, Japan; Andy Cubalit, CHS, Thailand; Daniel Cussen, Takushoku University, Japan; Le Dan, Ho Chi Minh City Electric Power College, Vietnam; Simon Daykin, Banghwa-dong Community Centre, South Korea; Aimee Denham, ILA, Vietnam; Bryan Dickson, David's English Center, Taipei; Nathan Ducker, Japan University, Japan; Ian Duncan, Simul International Corporate Training, Japan; Nguyen Thi Kieu Dung, Thang Long University, Vietnam; Truong Quang Dung, Tien Giang University, Vietnam; Nguyen Thi Thuy Duong, Vietnamese American Vocational Training College, Vietnam; Wong Tuck Ee, Raja Tun Azlan Science Secondary School, Malaysia; Emilia Effendy, International Islamic University Malaysia, Malaysia; Bettizza Escueta, KMUTT, Thailand; Robert Eva, Kaisei Girls High School, Japan; Jim George, Luna International Language School, Japan; Jurgen Germeys, Silk Road Language Center, South Korea; Wong Ai Gnoh, SMJK Chung Hwa Confucian, Malaysia; Sarah Go, Seoul Women's University, South Korea; Peter Goosselink, Hokkai High School, Japan; Robert Gorden, SNU, South Korea; Wendy M. Gough, St. Mary College/Nunoike Gaigo Senmon Gakko, Japan; Tim Grose, Sapporo Gakuin University, Japan; Pham Thu Ha, Le Van Tam Primary School, Vietnam; Ann-Marie Hadzima, Taipei; Troy Hammond, Tokyo Gakugei University International Secondary School, Japan; Robiatul 'Adawiah Binti Hamzah, SMK Putrajaya Precinct 8(1), Malaysia; Tran Thi Thuy Hang, Ho Chi Minh City Banking University, Vietnam; To Thi Hong Hanh, CEFALT, Vietnam; George Hays, Tokyo Kokusai Daigaku, Japan; Janis Hearn, Hongik University, South Korea; Chantel Hemmi, Jochi Daigaku, Japan; David Hindman, Sejong University, South Korea; Nahn Cam Hoa, Ho Chi Minh City University of Technology, Vietnam; Jana Holt, Korea University, South Korea; Jason Hollowell, Nihon University, Japan; F. N. (Zoe) Hsu, National Tainan University, Yong Kang; Kuei-ping Hsu, National Tsing Hua University, Hsinchu City; Wenhua Hsu, I-Shou University, Kaohsiung; Luu Nguyen Quoc Hung, Cantho University, Vietnam; Cecile Hwang, Changwon National University, South Korea; Ainol Haryati Ibrahim, Universiti Malaysia Pahang, Malaysia; Robert Jeens, Yonsei University, South Korea; Linda M. Joyce, Kyushu Sangyo University, Japan; Dr. Nisai Kaewsanchai, English Square Kanchanaburi, Thailand; Aniza Kamarulzaman, Sabah Science Secondary School, Malaysia; Ikuko Kashiwabara, Osaka Electro-Communication University, Japan; Gurmit Kaur, INTI College, Malaysia; Nick Keane, Japan; Ward Ketcheson, Aomori University, Japan; Nicholas Kemp, Kyushu International University, Japan; Montchatry Ketmuni, Rajamangala University of Technology, Thailand; Dinh Viet Khanh, Vietnam; Seonok Kim, Kangsu Jongro Language School, South Korea; Suyeon Kim, Anyang University, South Korea; Kelly P. Kimura, Soka University, Japan; Masakazu Kimura, Katoh Gakuen Gyoshu High School, Japan; Gregory King, Chubu Daigaku, Japan; Stan Kirk, Konan University, Japan; Donald Knight, Nan Hua/Fu Li Junior High Schools, Hsinchu; Kari J. Kostiainen, Nagoya City University, Japan; Pattri Kuanpulpol, Silpakorn University, Thailand; Ha Thi Lan, Thai Binh Teacher Training College, Vietnam; Eric Edwin Larson, Miyazaki Prefectural Nursing University, Japan; David Laurence, Chubu Daigaku, Japan; Richard S. Lavin, Prefectural University of Kumamoto, Japan; Shirley Leane, Chugoku Junior College, Japan; I-Hsiu Lee, Yunlin; Nari Lee, Park Jung PLS, South Korea; Tae Lee, Yonsei University, South Korea; Lys Yongsoon Lee, Reading Town Geumcheon, South Korea; Mallory Leece, Sun Moon University, South Korea; Dang Hong Lien, Tan Lam Upper Secondary School, Vietnam; Huang Li-Han, Rebecca Education Institute, Taipei; Sovannarith Lim, Royal University of Phnom Penh, Cambodia; Ginger Lin, National Kaohsiung Hospitality College, Kaohsiung; Noel Lineker, New Zealand/Japan; Tran Dang Khanh Linh, Nha Trang Teachers' Training College, Vietnam; Daphne Liu, Buliton English School, Taipei; S. F. Josephine Liu, Tien-Mu Elementary School, Taipei; Caroline Luo, Tunghai University, Taichung; Jeng-Jia Luo, Tunghai University, Taichung; Laura MacGregor, Gakushuin University, Japan; Amir Madani, Visuttharangsi School, Thailand; Elena Maeda, Sacred Heart Professional Training College, Japan; Vu Thi Thanh Mai, Hoang Gia Education Center, Vietnam; Kimura Masakazu, Kato Gakuen Gyoshu High School, Japan; Susumu Matsuhashi, Net Link English School, Japan; James McCrostie, Daito Bunka University, Japan; Joel McKee, Inha University, South Korea; Colin McKenzie, Wachirawit Primary School, Thailand; Terumi Miyazoe, Tokyo Denki Daigaku, Japan; William K. Moore, Hiroshima Kokusai Gakuin University, Japan; Kevin Mueller, Tokyo Kokusai Daigaku, Japan; Hudson Murrell, Baiko Gakuin University, Japan; Frances Namba, Senri International School of Kwansei Gakuin, Japan; Keiichi Narita, Niigata University, Japan; Kim Chung Nguyen, Ho Chi Minh University of

Industry, Vietnam; **Do Thi Thanh Nhan**, Hanoi University, Vietnam; **Dale Kazuo Nishi**, Aoyama English Conversation School, Japan; **Huynh Thi Ai Nguyen**, Vietnam; **Dongshin Oh**, YBM PLS, South Korea; **Keiko Okada**, Dokkyo Daigaku, Japan; **Louise Ohashi**, Shukutoku University, Japan; **Yongjun Park**, Sangji University, South Korea; **Donald Patnaude**, Ajarn Donald's English Language Services, Thailand; **Virginia Peng**, Ritsumeikan University, Japan; **Suangkanok Piboonthamnont**, Rajamangala University of Technology, Thailand; **Simon Pitcher**, Business English Teaching Services, Japan; **John C. Probert**, New Education Worldwide, Thailand; **Do Thi Hoa Quyen**, Ton Duc Thang University, Vietnam; **John P. Racine**, Dokkyo University, Japan; **Kevin Ramsden**, Kyoto University of Foreign Studies, Japan; **Luis Rappaport**, Cung Thieu Nha Ha Noi, Vietnam; **Lisa Reshad**, Konan Daigaku Hyogo, Japan; **Peter Riley**, Taisho University, Japan; **Thomas N. Robb**, Kyoto Sangyo University, Japan; **Rory Rosszell**, Meiji Daigaku, Japan; **Maria Feti Rosyani**, Universitas Kristen Indonesia, Indonesia; **Greg Rouault**, Konan University, Japan; **Chris Ruddenklau**, Kindai University, Japan; **Hans-Gustav Schwartz**, Thailand; **Mary-Jane Scott**, Soongsil University, South Korea; **Dara Sheahan**, Seoul National University, South Korea; **James Sherlock**, A.P.W. Angthong, Thailand; **Prof. Shieh**, Minghsin University of Science & Technology, Xinfeng; **Yuko Shimizu**, Ritsumeikan University, Japan; **Suzila Mohd Shukor**, Universiti Sains Malaysia, Malaysia; **Stephen E. Smith**, Mahidol University, Thailand; **Moon-young Son**, South Korea; **Seunghee Son**, Anyang University, South Korea; **Mi-young Song**, Kyungwon University, South Korea; **Lisa Sood**, VUS, BIS, Vietnam; **Jason Stewart**, Taejon International Language School, South Korea; **Brian A. Stokes**, Korea University, South Korea; **Mulder Su**, Shih-Chien University, Kaohsiung; **Yoomi Suh**, English Plus, South Korea; **Yun-Fang Sun**, Wenzao Ursuline College of Languages, Kaohsiung; **Richard Swingle**, Kansai Gaidai University, Japan; **Sanford Taborn**, Kinjo Gakuin Daigaku, Japan; **Mamoru Takahashi**, Akita Prefectural University, Japan; **Tran Hoang Tan**, School of International Training, Vietnam; **Takako Tanaka**, Doshisha University, Japan; **Jeffrey Taschner**, American University Alumni Language Center, Thailand; **Matthew Taylor**, Kinjo Gakuin Daigaku, Japan; **Michael Taylor**, International Pioneers School, Thailand; **Kampanart Thammaphati**, Wattana Wittaya Academy, Thailand; **Tran Duong The**, Sao Mai Language Center, Vietnam; **Tran Dinh Tho**, Duc Tri Secondary School, Vietnam; **Huynh Thi Anh Thu**, Nhatrang College of Culture Arts and Tourism, Vietnam; **Peter Timmins**, Peter's English School, Japan; **Fumie Togano**, Hosei Daini High School, Japan; **F. Sigmund Topor**, Keio University Language School, Japan; **Tu Trieu**, Rise VN, Vietnam; **Yen-Cheng Tseng**, Chang-Jung Christian University, Tainan; **Pei-Hsuan Tu**, National Cheng Kung University, Tainan City; **Hajime Uematsu**, Hirosaki University, Japan; **Rachel Um**, Mok-dong Oedae English School, South Korea; **David Underhill**, EEExpress, Japan; **Ben Underwood**, Kugenuma High School, Japan; **Siriluck Usaha**, Sripatum University, Thailand; **Tyas Budi Utami**, Indonesia; **Nguyen Thi Van**, Far East International School, Vietnam; **Stephan Van Eycken**, Kosei Gakuen Girls High School, Japan; **Zisa Velasquez**, Taihu International School/Semarang International School, China/ Indonesia; **Jeffery Walter**, Sangji University, South Korea; **Bill White**, Kinki University, Japan; **Yohanes De Deo Widyastoko**, Xaverius Senior High School, Indonesia; **Dylan Williams**, SNU, South Korea; **Jisuk Woo**, Ichean University, South Korea; **Greg Chung-Hsien Wu**, Providence University, Taichung; **Xun Xiaoming**, BLCU, China; **Hui-Lien Yeh**, Chai Nan University of Pharmacy and Science, Tainan; **Sittiporn Yodnil**, Huachiew Chalermprakiet University, Thailand; **Shamshul Helmy Zambahari**, Universiti Teknologi Malaysia, Malaysia; **Ming-Yuli**, Chang Jung Christian University, Tainan; **Aimin Fadhlee bin Mahmud Zuhodi**, Kuala Terengganu Science School, Malaysia;

TURKEY **Shirley F. Akis**, American Culture Association/Fomara; **Gül Akkoç**, Boğaziçi University; **Seval Akmeşe**, Haliç University; **Ayşenur Akyol**, Ege University; **Ayşe Umut Aribaş**, Beykent University; **Gökhan Asan**, Kapadokya Vocational College; **Hakan Asan**, Kapadokya Vocational College; **Julia Asan**, Kapadokya Vocational College; **Azarvan Atac**, Piri Reis University; **Nur Babat**, Kapadokya Vocational College; **Feyza Balakbabalar**, Kadir Has University; **Gözde Balikçi**, Beykent University; **Deniz Balım**, Haliç University; **Asli Başdoğan**, Kadir Has University; **Ayla Bayram**, Kapadokya Vocational College; **Pinar Bilgiç**, Kadir Has University; **Kenan Bozkurt**, Kapadokya Vocational College; **Yonca Bozkurt**, Ege University; **Frank Carr**, Piri Reis; **Mengü Noyan Çengel**, Ege University; **Elif Doğan**, Ege University; **Natalia Donmez**, 29 Mayis Üniversite; **Nalan Emirsoy**, Kadir Has University; **Ayşe Engin**, Kadir Has University; **Ayhan Gedikbaş**, Ege University; **Gülşah Gençer**, Beykent University; **Seyit Ömer Gök**, Gediz University; **Tuğba Gök**, Gediz University; **İlkay Gökçe**, Ege University; **Zeynep Birinci Guler**, Maltepe University; **Neslihan Güler**, Kadir Has University; **Sircan Gümüş**,

Kadir Has University; **Nesrin Gündoğu**, T.C. Piri Reis University; **Tanju Gurpinar**, Piri Reis University; **Selin Gurturk**, Piri Reis University; **Neslihan Gurutku**, Piri Reis University; **Roger Hewitt**, Maltepe University; **Nilüfer İbrahimoğlu**, Beykent University; **Nevin Kaftelen**, Kadir Has University; **Sultan Kalin**, Kapadokya Vocational College; **Sema Kaplan Karabina**, Anadolu University; **Eray Kara**, Giresun University; **Beylü Karayazgan**, Ege University; **Darren Kelso**, Piri Reis University; **Trudy Kittle**, Kapadokya Vocational College; **Şaziye Konaç**, Kadir Has University; **Güneş Korkmaz**, Kapadokya Vocational College; **Robert Ledbury**, Izmir University of Economics; **Ashley Lucas**, Maltepe University; **Bülent Nedium Uça**, Dogus University; **Murat Nurlu**, Ege University; **Mollie Owens**, Kadir Has University; **Oya Özağaç**, Boğaziçi University; **Funda Özcan**, Ege University; **İlkay Özdemir**, Ege University; **Ülkü Öztürk**, Gediz University; **Cassondra Puls**, Anadolu University; **Yelda Sarikaya**, Cappadocia Vocational College; **Müge Şekercioğlu**, Ege University; **Melis Senol**, Canakkale Onsekiz Mart University, The School of Foreign Languages; **Patricia Sümer**, Kadir Has University; **Rex Surface**, Beykent University; **Mustafa Torun**, Kapadokya Vocational College; **Tansel Üstünloğlu**, Ege University; **Fatih Yücel**, Beykent University; **Şule Yüksel**, Ege University;

THE MIDDLE EAST **Amina Saif Mohammed Al Hashamia**, Nizwa College of Applied Sciences, Oman; **Jennifer Baran**, Kuwait University, Kuwait; **Phillip Chappells**, GEMS Modern Academy, U.A.E.; **Sharon Ruth Devaneson**, Ibri College of Technology, Oman; **Hanaa El-Deeb**, Canadian International College, Egypt; **Yvonne Eaton**, Community College of Qatar, Qatar; **Brian Gay**, Sultan Qaboos University, Oman; **Gail Al Hafidh**, Sharjah Women's College (HCT), U.A.E.; **Jonathan Hastings**, American Language Center, Jordan; **Laurie Susan Hilu**, English Language Centre, University of Bahrain, Bahrain; **Abraham Irannezhad**, Mehre Aval, Iran; **Kevin Kempe**, CNA-Q, Qatar; **Jill Newby James**, University of Nizwa; **Mary Kay Klein**, American University of Sharjah, U.A.E.; **Sian Khoury**, Fujairah Women's College (HCT), U.A.E.; **Hussein Dehghan Manshadi**, Farhang Pajooh & Jaam-e-Jam Language School, Iran; **Jessica March**, American University of Sharjah, U.A.E.; **Neil McBeath**, Sultan Qaboos University, Oman; **Sandy McDonagh**, Abu Dhabi Men's College (HCT), U.A.E.; **Rob Miles**, Sharjah Women's College (HCT), U.A.E.; **Michael Kevin Neumann**, Al Ain Men's College (HCT), U.A.E.;

LATIN AMERICA **Aldana Aguirre**, Argentina; **Claudia Almeida**, Coordenação de Idiomas, Brazil; **Cláudia Arias**, Brazil; **Maria de los Angeles Barba**, FES Acatlan UNAM, Mexico; **Lilia Barrios**, Universidad Autónoma de Tamaulipas, Mexico; **Adán Beristain**, UAEM, Mexico; **Ricardo Böck**, Manoel Ribas, Brazil; **Edson Braga**, CNA, Brazil; **Marli Buttelli**, Mater et Magistra, Brazil; **Alessandra Campos**, Inova Centro de Linguas, Brazil; **Priscila Catta Preta Ribeiro**, Brazil; **Gustavo Cestari**, Access International School, Brazil; **Walter D'Alessandro**, Virginia Language Center, Brazil; **Lilian De Gennaro**, Argentina; **Mônica De Stefani**, Quality Centro de Idiomas, Brazil; **Julio Alejandro Flores**, BUAP, Mexico; **Mirian Freire**, CNA Vila Guilherme, Brazil; **Francisco Garcia**, Colegio Lestonnac de San Angel, Mexico; **Miriam Giovanardi**, Brazil; **Darlene Gonzalez Miy**, ITESM CCV, Mexico; **Maria Laura Grimaldi**, Argentina; **Luz Dary Guzmán**, IMPAHU, Colombia; **Carmen Koppe**, Brazil; **Monica Krutzler**, Brazil; **Marcus Murilo Lacerda**, Seven Idiomas, Brazil; **Nancy Lake**, CEL LEP, Brazil; **Cris Lazzcrini**, Brazil; **Sandra Luna**, Argentina; **Ricardo Luvisan**, Brazil; **Jorge Murilo Menezes**, ACBEU, Brazil; **Monica Navarro**, Instituto Cultural A. C., Mexico; **Joacyr Oliveira**, Faculdades Metropolitanas Unidas and Summit School for Teachers, Brazil; **Ayrton Cesar Oliveira de Araujo**, E&A English Classes, Brazil; **Ana Laura Oriente**, Seven Idiomas, Brazil; **Adelia Peña Clavel**, CELE UNAM, Mexico; **Beatriz Pereira**, Summit School, Brazil; **Miguel Perez**, Instituto Cultural, Mexico; **Cristiane Perone**, Associação Cultura Inglesa, Brazil; **Pamela Claudia Pogré**, Colegio Integral Caballito / Universidad de Flores, Argentina; **Dalva Prates**, Brazil; **Marianne Rampaso**, Iowa Idiomas, Brazil; **Daniela Rutolo**, Instituto Superior Cultural Británico, Argentina; **Maione Sampaio**, Maione Carrijo Consultoria em Inglês Ltda, Brazil; **Elaine Santesso**, TS Escola de Idiomas, Brazil; **Camila Francisco Santos**, UNS Idiomas, Brazil; **Lucia Silva**, Cooplem Idiomas, Brazil; **Maria Adela Sorzio**, Instituto Superior Santa Cecilia, Argentina; **Elcio Souza**, Unibero, Brazil; **Willie Thomas**, Rainbow Idiomas, Brazil; **Sandra Villegas**, Instituto Humberto de Paolis, Argentina; **John Whelan**, La Universidad Nacional Autonoma de Mexico, Mexico

CONTENTS

UNIT 1

Sociology

NOTE TAKING ▶	using notes to summarize a lecture
LISTENING ▶	making inferences
VOCABULARY ▶	suffixes
GRAMMAR ▶	auxiliary verbs *do, be, have*
PRONUNCIATION ▶	contractions with auxiliary verbs
SPEAKING ▶	taking conversational turns

UNIT QUESTION

Are first impressions accurate?

A Discuss these questions with your classmates.

1. What do you notice when you meet someone for the first time?

2. How important do you think first impressions are? Why?

3. Look at the photo. What do you think of this person from just looking at him? Do you think your first impression is accurate? Why or why not?

B Listen to *The Q Classroom* online. Then answer these questions.

1. How did the students answer the question? Do you agree or disagree with their ideas? Why?

2. What are some other ways that a person can give a good impression? What are some ways that a person can give a bad impression?

iQ ONLINE **C** Go to the Online Discussion Board to discuss the Unit Question with your classmates.

UNIT
OBJECTIVE

Listen to a lecture and an excerpt from a radio show and gather information and ideas to describe in detail an accurate first impression.

D Read the proverbs (sayings). Decide whether each proverb means that first impressions are *accurate* (**A**) or *not accurate* (**N**). Discuss your answers with a partner. Look up any unfamiliar words in the dictionary.

_____ 1. Don't judge a horse by its saddle. (Arabic)

_____ 2. Faces we see; hearts we don't know. (Spanish)

_____ 3. What you see is what you get. (English)

_____ 4. You must judge a man by the work of his hands. (African)

_____ 5. Never judge a book by its cover. (English)

_____ 6. A tree starts with a seed. (Arabic)

_____ 7. If it walks like a duck and quacks like a duck, it's a duck. (English)

_____ 8. Don't think there are no crocodiles because the water is calm. (Malaysian)

E Do you have any proverbs in your culture about first impressions? What are they? Tell your partner.

F Which proverbs from Activity D do you think are the truest? Discuss your ideas with your partner.

A good way to remember a lecture is to put the key ideas into your own words. This will also help you confirm that you understood all the information and that your notes are complete.

As soon as possible after a lecture, put the key, or most important, ideas into your own words, and say them out loud to a study partner or to yourself. Saying them out loud will help you clarify the ideas and remember them better.

Imagine this situation: Your friend had to miss class because he was ill. The next day, he asks you to tell him about the lecture. What would you tell him?

You would probably give him the following information:

- the topic of the lecture
- the main ideas
- a few important points and examples

This is the same information that you use when you summarize. A **summary** is a shorter version of the information that includes all of the main ideas, but only a few details.

Here are some phrases that are used as signposts.

- *The professor talked about . . .*
- *She explained . . .*
- *She told us . . .*
- *Then he discussed . . .*
- *He gave us the example of . . .*
- *After that he wrapped up with . . .*

A. Read this excerpt from a lecture on first impressions. Then answer the questions.

When you meet someone for the first time, you want to be remembered in a positive way. One way to make a good first impression is to listen. Sometimes speakers talk too much and don't listen. Show interest and ask questions. What does the other person like to do? Where is he or she from? What is his or her family like?

Second, use body language effectively. What does this mean? Show you are paying attention by leaning in, maintaining eye contact, and using facial expressions. Smile, raise your eyebrows, and tilt your head. Through your use of questions and body language, you can make a good first impression.

1. What is the topic? _____

2. What two main points does the speaker make?

   _____

   _____

3. What is one detail that illustrates each main point?

   _____

   _____

B. With a partner, take turns summarizing the lecture excerpt.

C. Go online for more practice using notes to summarize a lecture.

LISTENING

LISTENING 1 | The Psychology of First Impressions

 You are going to listen to a lecture about first impressions. As you listen to the lecture, gather information and ideas about first impressions.

PREVIEW THE LISTENING

 **Tip** for Success

Presentations and talks often begin with a short story or anecdote. The story is usually an example of the topic the speaker is going to talk about.

A. PREVIEW A psychologist will explain how first impressions affect our opinion of a new person. Check (✓) the statement about first impressions you think is true.

☐ First impressions give us a good idea of what a person is really like.

☐ We often make errors because of first impressions.

B. VOCABULARY Read aloud these words from Listening 1. Check (✓) the ones you know. Use a dictionary to define any new or unknown words. Then discuss with a partner how the words will relate to the unit.

assume (v.) 🔑	form an impression (phr.)
behavior (n.) 🔑	negative (adj.) 🔑
briefly (adv.) 🔑	positive (adj.) 🔑
encounter (n.) 🔑	sample (n.) 🔑
error (n.) 🔑	trait (n.)

🔑 Oxford 3000™ words

iQ ONLINE **C.** Go online to listen and practice your pronunciation.

WORK WITH THE LISTENING

A. LISTEN AND TAKE NOTES Listen to the lecture about first impressions. Before you listen, look at the outline below. As you listen, add the topic and important details.

Topic: _____

Example: Waiting in line at a coffee shop

Main idea: Impressions of others

Detail(s)

First mistake: _____

Second mistake: _____

Main idea: When we view our own behavior

Detail: It's not our personality; it's the _____.

B. **Work with a partner. Take turns using your notes to summarize the lecture.**

C. **Read the statements. Write _T_ (true) or _F_ (false). Then correct each false statement to make it true.**

1. _F_ First impressions tell the whole story.

   First impressions tell only part of the story. _____

2. ___ If a person is happy when we meet her, we will often think she is happy all the time.

   _____

3. ___ Our first impressions give us an accurate picture of the whole person.

   _____

4. ___ We judge other people's behavior differently from our own.

   _____

D. **Read the sentences. Then listen again. Circle the answer or answers that best complete each statement.**

1. People _____ what they see in a first encounter.
   a. often make mistakes about
   b. make sense of information from
   c. form very accurate impressions from

2. People assume that their first impressions tell them about _____ person.
   a. a sample of a
   b. most of a
   c. the whole

3. If we think a person is happy when we first meet her, we will think she is also _____.
   a. friendly
   b. boring
   c. kind

4. If someone else does something negative, we think _____.

   a. it is because of his personality

   b. he is a bad person

   c. it is because of how he felt that day

5. If we do something negative, we think it is because of _____.

   a. our personality

   b. the situation

   c. someone else

E. Check (✓) the statements you think the lecturer agrees with. Discuss your answers with a partner. Support your arguments with information from the lecture.

☐ 1. If a stranger behaves rudely, you may assume he isn't intelligent.

☐ 2. First impressions are rarely accurate.

☐ 3. People make more excuses for their own bad behavior.

☐ 4. An example of behavior can tell us a lot about someone's personality.

F. Read the text below. Discuss the questions with a partner.

On my first day of college, I was moving into my dorm room when my roommate, Renee, came in. She had already moved in and taken the bed by the window. Her stuff was everywhere. Her parents were with her. They were very nice and introduced themselves, but Renee was quiet and didn't really look at me. I didn't say much either because I thought she didn't like me. She threw her bag on her bed and they all left. I was very upset. I thought Renee was rude and mean. I was mad that she didn't even give me a chance.

An hour or so later, Renee came back to the room. She apologized for her rudeness. She had just had a bad argument with her parents and was upset with them. She described their fight in a very funny way, and we both laughed. After that, she became one of my best friends. She's the perfect roommate.

1. How accurate was the writer's first impression of her roommate?

2. How does this story illustrate the points the speaker made in her lecture?

G. Go online to listen to *First Impressions from Photos* and check your comprehension.

 for Success

Pay attention to articles. They come before nouns and help you identify parts of speech.

H. VOCABULARY Use the new vocabulary from Listening 1. Complete each sentence with the correct word or phrase.

assume *(v.)*	error *(n.)*	positive *(adj.)*
behavior *(n.)*	form an impression *(phr.)*	sample *(n.)*
briefly *(adv.)*	negative *(adj.)*	trait *(n.)*
encounter *(n.)*		

1. I took a(n) _____ of the carpet home to see whether I liked the color in my living room.

2. Alberto made several _____ on his math test because he didn't study hard enough.

3. Luisa said she wasn't feeling well, so I _____ she's not going out tonight.

4. The teacher went over yesterday's assignment very _____. We only spent about fifteen minutes on it, so I still have some questions.

5. When I meet new people, I watch their _____ closely to see what they are like.

6. It only takes a few minutes to _____ of someone you meet for the first time.

7. One _____ thing about moving to a new place is leaving your friends and family behind.

8. Most of my good friends have one personality _____ in common—they are all very funny.

9. Do you usually have a(n) _____ feeling about people when you meet them for the first time? I do because I think most people are good.

10. My first _____ with my new neighbors was very unpleasant. We argued about the amount of noise they were making.

iQ ONLINE **I.** Go online for more practice with the vocabulary.

 SAY WHAT YOU THINK

Discuss the questions in a group.

1. In this lecture, the speaker says we often think that the way a person behaves when we first meet him is the way he behaves all the time. From your personal experience, do you agree or disagree? Give examples.

2. Have you ever formed a first impression of someone that was wrong? Explain.

Making inferences means to draw conclusions about information that is not stated directly by using information that you already know or that is stated directly. Making inferences while listening can help deepen your understanding of what you hear.

Listen to a student talking about meeting his professor for the first time.

> When I first met my professor, he shook my hand firmly and then asked me questions about myself. He was very polite. He also was relaxed and seemed interested in what I was saying.

Even though the student does not state directly that his first impression of his professor was positive, you can infer or conclude that he did from the information he does state directly.

- He shook my hand firmly.
- He asked questions.
- He was relaxed and seemed interested.

A. Listen to a student talk about a first impression. Take notes in your notebook as you listen. Then answer the questions.

1. Do you think it was a positive or negative first impression? Why? What information from your notes helped you answer?

   _____

2. Do you think the speaker likes Lee? Why? What information from your notes helped you answer?

   _____

B. Work with a partner. Compare your answers.

C. Listen to the speaker's opinion of Lee. Take notes in your notebook. Compare what the speaker says about Lee with your answers in Activity A.

D. Work with a partner. Tell a story about meeting someone for the first time. Describe what she or he did and a few things you noticed. Don't say how you felt about the person. Ask your partner to infer whether your impression was positive or negative.

iQ ONLINE **E.** Go online for more practice making inferences.

LISTENING 2 | Book Review of *Blink* by Malcolm Gladwell

You are going to listen to an excerpt from a radio show in which a critic reviews a book. The book discusses the types of decisions we make as a result of first impressions. As you listen to the excerpt, gather information and ideas about first impressions.

PREVIEW THE LISTENING

A. **PREVIEW** Check (✓) which things, if any, you could easily make a quick decision about.

☐ a book to read   ☐ a new pair of shoes
☐ a DVD to watch   ☐ a place to go on vacation
☐ a new car   ☐ a restaurant

B. **VOCABULARY** Read aloud these words from Listening 2. Check (✓) the ones you know. Use a dictionary to define any new or unknown words. Then discuss with a partner how the words will relate to the unit.

conscious *(adj.)* 🔑	reliable *(adj.)*
effective *(adj.)* 🔑	select *(v.)* 🔑
expert *(n.)* 🔑	snap judgment *(phr.)*
fake *(n.)*	suspicious *(adj.)* 🔑
instinct *(n.)*	unconsciously *(adv.)*

🔑 Oxford 3000™ words

iQ ONLINE **C.** Go online to listen and practice your pronunciation.

WORK WITH THE LISTENING

A. **LISTEN AND TAKE NOTES** Listen to the book review of *Blink* by Malcolm Gladwell. Before you listen, look at the partial outline below. As you listen, take notes on the main ideas, examples, and other details. After the listening is over, go back and add to or edit your notes for clarity.

Topic: Malcolm Gladwell's *Blink*

Main idea: Gladwell thinks first impressions are usually _____.

Example:

Two ways we make decisions

1. _____ with our conscious minds

2. quickly, or _____

Research on accurate first impressions

Students watched videos of _____ , could tell

how _____ they would be.

People could look at _____ and learn

about _____ .

Examples of decision-making

Careful: _____

Snap: _____

B. With a partner, take turns summarizing the review from your notes.

C. Complete the chart. Use your notes from activity A. Compare charts with a partner.

Main ideas	Examples or details
First impressions are _____ .	
Unconscious decisions are _____ .	
Conscious decisions are _____ .	

D. Listen again. Match each detail with an example given in the review. Then put the details in the order you heard them.

Examples
a. selecting a soccer player
b. looking at a bedroom
c. buying something for the kitchen
d. watching a video
e. writing down the first word that comes to mind

Details   Order you heard in the report

____ an easy decision   ____

____ describing someone's character   ____

____ recognizing a fake artifact   1

____ judging a teacher's effectiveness   ____

____ a difficult decision with a lot of information ____

E. Read each situation. Based on the book review, do you think you should use your instincts and make a snap judgment (unconscious), or make a careful list of good and bad points (conscious)? Write *U* or *C*. Explain your reasons to a partner.

1. buying a coffee maker ____

2. choosing a study partner ____

3. asking someone on the street for help ____

4. choosing vegetable seeds for your garden ____

5. buying a car ____

6. choosing a seat on a train ____

F. Read more information below on first impressions from two researchers. With a partner, discuss five tips you can give others on making first impressions. Use this information and the information from *Blink*.

Nalini Ambady was a researcher at Tufts University. She did a study on how well students could make judgments about instructors from a short video. According to Ambady, when people think more before making a decision, the decisions tend not to be as good as when they make them unconsciously.

Frank Bernieri of Oregon State University says that research suggests that people who are more confident about their judgments of people are actually less accurate. He advises people to try to convince themselves of the opposite point of view. For example, if you assume someone is rude and unkind, you should try to see his or her behavior in a completely different way.

Tips:

_____

_____

_____

_____

_____

G. **VOCABULARY** Use the new vocabulary from Listening 2. Read the sentences. Circle the answer that best matches the meaning of each bold word or phrase.

1. I make a **conscious** effort to stay in regular contact with all my friends. I make time to call and email them often.
   a. accidental   b. intentional   c. occasional

2. Watching a video is an **effective** way to study someone's behavior. You can learn a lot from the way people move their hands.
   a. successful   b. interesting   c. unusual

3. Marcos is an **expert** at swimming. He has been doing it a long time.
   a. beginner   b. failure   c. skillful person

4. The artifact was a **fake**. It was not thousands of years old.
   a. an imitation   b. a problem   c. an original

5. When you meet new people, you should trust your **instincts**. Your first reaction is often correct.
   a. natural feelings   b. general knowledge   c. careful research

6. My car isn't **reliable**. There is always something wrong with it.
   a. dependable   b. expensive   c. comfortable

7. I can't **select** anyone to receive the award. There are too many good students.
   a. tell   b. call   c. choose

8. I often make **snap judgments** about things I buy. I don't like to waste time.
   a. careful decisions   b. bad decisions   c. quick decisions

9. My parents were **suspicious** when I told them the teacher did not give any grades for our assignment.
   a. uninterested   b. doubtful   c. excited

10. I was so focused on listening to the news this morning that I **unconsciously** poured orange juice in my coffee instead of milk.
    a. without thinking   b. without caring   c. without studying

iQ ONLINE **H.** Go online for more practice with the vocabulary.

SAY WHAT YOU THINK

A. Discuss the questions in a group.

1. Malcolm Gladwell suggests that we should make difficult decisions more quickly and with our unconscious minds. Do you agree with him? Why or why not?

2. According to Gladwell, our first impressions are often reliable. Do you think this is true? Why or why not?

B. Before you watch the video, discuss the questions in a group.

1. In which situations are first impressions really important?

2. How do you want to present yourself in a job interview?

iQ ONLINE

C. Go online to watch a video about the mistakes people make in a job interview. Then check your comprehension.

> **VIDEO VOCABULARY**
>
> **err on the conservative side** *(phr.)* to choose to be too cautious rather than too casual
>
> **grievance** *(n.)* something you complain about
>
> **mind-boggling** *(adj.)* very difficult to imagine or understand
>
> **on point** *(adj.)* appropriate or relevant to the situation
>
> **upper hand** *(n.)* an advantage

 Critical Thinking **Tip**

Activity D asks you to **compare** and **contrast** job interviews with other types of first impressions. You compare ideas that are the same. You contrast ideas that are different. **Comparing** and **contrasting** can help you understand the ways in which job interviews are similar to or different from other types of first impressions.

D. Think about the unit video, Listening 1, and Listening 2 as you discuss the questions.

1. In what kinds of situations do you think first impressions are usually accurate?

2. In what ways are job interviews similar to other types of first impressions people make? How are they different?

We form first impressions wherever we are.

Use **suffixes** and other word endings to help you recognize parts of speech. Recognizing the part of speech will help you guess the meaning of an unfamiliar word. It will also help you expand your vocabulary as you notice other parts of speech in the same word family.

Common noun suffixes: *-acy, -er/-or, -ment, -ness, -tion*

    accur**acy**, research**er**, invent**or**, amuse**ment**, friendli**ness**, atten**tion**

Common verb suffixes: *-ate, -en, -ize*

    stimul**ate**, strength**en**, energ**ize**

Common adjective suffixes: *-able, al, ful, -ive, -ous*

    depend**able**, tradition**al**, care**ful**, effect**ive**, humor**ous**

Common adverb suffixes: *-ly, -ally*

    particular**ly**, univers**ally**

A. Look at the new words. For each word, write the suffix, the part of speech, and the base word from which the new word is formed.

New word	Suffix	Part of speech	Base word
1. accuracy	-acy	noun	accurate
2. assumption			
3. consciously			
4. prediction			
5. effectively			
6. instinctive			
7. selection			

B. Work with a partner. Discuss the meanings of the new words from Activity A. Then use a dictionary to check the definitions of any words you are not sure of.

C. **Complete each sentence with the correct word from Activity A.**

1. That bookstore offers a great _____ of classic literature. There are so many, it's hard to choose!

2. _____ is really important in grammar, so you should try not to make mistakes.

3. We often make _____ about people because of the way they look. Then we sometimes discover that our first impressions were incorrect.

4. I don't pay much attention to weather reports. Their _____ are usually wrong. It was supposed to be sunny yesterday, but it rained all day!

5. If an advertisement is _____ designed, sales of the product will increase.

6. Many animals have a(n) _____ fear of fire and the danger it represents. They don't learn it. It's part of their nature.

7. I have to make decisions very _____ when I go shopping. If I don't, I buy things I really don't need without even realizing it.

 **D.** Go online for more practice with suffixes.

SPEAKING

UNIT OBJECTIVE ▶▶▶▶ At the end of this unit, you will give a short talk to a partner about a first impression. Make sure to take conversational turns when you talk to your partner.

| Grammar | Auxiliary verbs *do, be, have* |

The **auxiliary verbs** *do*, *be*, and *have* are used to make questions and negative statements.

Use *do* with the simple present and simple past.

Simple present	**Simple past**
Does he like pizza?	**Did** they bring their books?
He **doesn't** like pizza.	They **didn't** bring their books.

Use *be* with the present and past continuous.

Present continuous	**Past continuous**
Are you reading?	**Was** Mr. Knight teaching here last year?
We **aren't** reading now.	He **wasn't** teaching here last year.

Use *have* with the present perfect.

Present perfect
Has she left yet?
Nancy **hasn't** left yet.

A. Rewrite the sentences as negative statements. Use the correct form of *do, be,* or *have* as the auxiliary verb.

1. I often make snap judgments.

   I don't often make snap judgments.

2. Bill thinks first impressions about teachers are usually accurate.

   _____

3. Sara trusted her instincts when meeting new people.

   _____

4. When Waleed buys something, he usually thinks about it for a long time.

   _____

5. Jenny is working hard this week.

_____

6. I've formed a positive impression of that company.

_____

B. Rewrite the sentences as questions. Use the correct form of *do, be,* or *have* as the auxiliary verb.

1. You have made many incorrect assumptions because of how someone looked.

   Have you made many incorrect assumptions because of how someone looked?

2. I like talking to new people on the phone.

   _____

3. Ross is living with people he met last year.

   _____

4. Hatem made lots of friends at school.

   _____

5. The experts realized the artifact was a fake.

   _____

6. Jamal has selected his library books already.

   _____

C. Work with a partner. Take turns asking and answering the questions from Activity B. Use auxiliary verbs in your short answers.

   A: Do you like talking to new people on the phone?
   B: Yes, I do./No, I don't.

D. Go online for more practice with auxiliary verbs.

E. Go online for the grammar expansion.

Contractions with auxiliary verbs

Auxiliary verbs are usually unstressed and can be shortened as part of a **contraction**. Most contractions can be used in speech and informal writing, but some are only used in speech.

Listen to these examples of contractions.

Contractions used in speech or writing

> She's eating now. (She is eating now.)
> They're watching TV. (They are watching TV.)
> Lisa's already left. (Lisa has already left.)
> We've finished our work. (We have finished our work.)

Contractions used only in speech

> What's it cost? (What does it cost?)
> Where'd you go? (Where did you go?)
> Why'd he arrive so late? (Why did he arrive so late?)

A. Listen to these sentences with contractions. Write the full form of the auxiliary verb.

1. Who _____ your favorite author?

2. Where _____ you go on your last vacation?

3. Mary _____ going to the store.

4. Jack _____ gone already.

5. We _____ usually eaten by 6:00.

6. What _____ you do after class yesterday?

7. The girls _____ been here before.

B. Work with a partner. Take turns saying the sentences from Activity A. Use the full form of the auxiliary verbs. Then practice saying them with contractions.

iQ ONLINE **C.** Go online for more practice with contractions with auxiliary verbs.

When you are speaking with someone, it is polite to take turns talking. Taking turns keeps the conversation going and shows that you are interested in what the other person is saying.

If the other person asks you a question, answer it, and add some new information. If possible, ask a question of your own. Here are some questions you can use.

What do you think?	How about you?
Do you agree?	You know?
Right?	OK?

A. Complete the conversation with questions from the Speaking Skill box. Then practice the conversation with a partner.

Tony: Hi. I'm Tony. It's nice to meet you.

Alex: My name's Alex. Nice to meet you too. Are you a new student?

Tony: No. I've been studying here for two years.

_____
1

Alex: I just started this week, but so far, this class looks interesting.

_____
2

Tony: I agree. The teacher's very effective. The book he's using looks good, too.

_____
3

Alex: Yeah. He seems friendly and interesting.

B. Read the questions and write notes in your notebook to help you answer. Then have a conversation about each question with a partner. Keep the conversations going for at least three turns each, and signal your partner's turn by using questions from the Speaking Skill box.

1. Who was your most effective teacher when you were a child? What impressed you about him or her?

2. Have you ever made a bad first impression on someone else? What did you do?

iQ ONLINE   **C.** Go online for more practice with taking conversational turns.

UNIT
OBJECTIVE ▶▶▶▶

In this assignment, you are going to give a talk to a partner about a first impression. As you prepare your talk, think about the Unit Question, "Are first impressions accurate?" Use information from Listening 1, Listening 2, the unit video, and your work in this unit to support your talk. Refer to the Self-Assessment checklist on page 24.

CONSIDER THE IDEAS

Which items in the chart tell you the most about new people when you are forming a first impression? Check (✓) whether you think each item is very important, important, or not important. Then compare and discuss your answers with a partner.

	Very important	Important	Not important
their level of politeness	☐	☐	☐
their clothing	☐	☐	☐
their hairstyle	☐	☐	☐
their voice	☐	☐	☐
their eye contact	☐	☐	☐
their attitude to money	☐	☐	☐
the way they drive	☐	☐	☐
their job	☐	☐	☐
their likes and dislikes	☐	☐	☐
Your own ideas:			
	☐	☐	☐
	☐	☐	☐

PREPARE AND SPEAK

A. GATHER IDEAS Complete these steps.

1. Think about a time when your first impression of someone was incorrect.

2. Brainstorm as much as you can remember about the situation.

3. Then write what you thought about the person when you first met and how your first impression was wrong.

B. ORGANIZE IDEAS Use your ideas from Activity A to help you answer these questions. Do not write full sentences. Just write notes to help you remember your answers.

Who was the person? _____

Where, when, and why did you meet? _____

What was your first impression? _____

Why did you form this impression? _____

When did you realize your first impression was wrong? _____

What changed your mind? _____

What do you think about the person now? _____

C. SPEAK Tell your partner about your first impression of the person you chose. Refer to the Self-Assessment checklist before you begin.

1. Explain why you formed that impression and why you were wrong.

2. You can refer to your notes, but do not read exactly what you wrote.

3. Talk for at least one minute.

iQ ONLINE **Go online for your alternate Unit Assignment.**

CHECK AND REFLECT

A. CHECK Think about the Unit Assignment as you complete the Self-Assessment checklist.

Yes	No	SELF-ASSESSMENT
☐	☐	I was able to speak easily about the topic.
☐	☐	My partner understood me.
☐	☐	I used vocabulary from the unit.
☐	☐	I used auxiliary verbs and contractions.
☐	☐	I took turns when speaking.

B. REFLECT Go to the Online Discussion Board to discuss these questions.

1. What is something new you learned in this unit?

2. Look back at the Unit Question—Are first impressions accurate? Is your answer different now than when you started this unit? If yes, how is it different? Why?

TRACK YOUR SUCCESS

Circle the words and phrases you have learned in this unit.

Nouns
accuracy AWL
assumption AWL
behavior 🔑
encounter 🔑 AWL
error 🔑 AWL
expert 🔑 AWL
fake
instinct
prediction AWL
sample 🔑
selection 🔑 AWL
trait

Verbs
assume 🔑 AWL
select 🔑 AWL

Adjectives
conscious 🔑
effective 🔑
instinctive
negative 🔑 AWL
positive 🔑 AWL
reliable AWL
suspicious 🔑

Adverbs
briefly 🔑 AWL
consciously
unconsciously

Phrases
form an impression
snap judgment
Do you agree?
How about you?
OK?
Right?
What do you think?
You know?

🔑 Oxford 3000™ words
AWL Academic Word List

Check (✓) the skills you learned. If you need more work on a skill, refer to the page(s) in parentheses.

NOTE TAKING	☐ I can use my notes to summarize a lecture. (p. 5)
LISTENING	☐ I can make inferences. (p. 11)
VOCABULARY	☐ I can use suffixes. (p. 17)
GRAMMAR	☐ I can use the auxiliary verbs *do*, *be*, and *have*. (p. 19)
PRONUNCIATION	☐ I can use contractions with auxiliary verbs. (p. 21)
SPEAKING	☐ I can take conversational turns. (p. 22)
UNIT OBJECTIVE ▶▶▶▶	☐ I can gather information and ideas to describe in detail an accurate first impression.

UNIT QUESTION

What's more important: taste or nutrition?

A Discuss these questions with your classmates.

1. How important is food in your life? Do you "eat to live" or "live to eat"?

2. Do you agree that if something tastes great, it's probably bad for you?

3. Look at the photo. What can you tell about these people's attitude about food and nutrition?

UNIT
OBJECTIVE ▶▶▶▶ Listen to an interview and a talk and gather
information and ideas to conduct a class survey
on food preferences.

🔊 **B** Listen to *The Q Classroom* online. Then
match the ideas in the box to the students.

a. we need food that is both healthy and tastes good
b. ~~eating healthy food is important~~
c. good nutrition makes people healthy
d. food that tastes good makes people happy

The importance of taste and nutrition	
Sophy	b. eating healthy food is important
Felix	
Marcus	
Yuna	

 C Go to the Online Discussion Board to discuss the Unit Question with
your classmates.

D Read the paragraph and complete the chart.

A Matter of Taste

For a long time, experts in the West believed there were only four basic tastes: *sweet, sour, salty,* and *bitter*. Then, in the early 2000s, *umami* was recognized as the fifth basic taste. *Umami* is a Japanese word that means "yummy" or "nice." It describes food that tastes "meaty," such as meat, fish, and cheese.

bananas

ice cream

pickle

nuts

grapefruit

coffee

radish

lemon

> Look at the pictures. Where do you think each food or drink should go? Complete the chart. Then check (✓) your favorite foods.

parsley

pineapple

chicken

potato chips

Sweet	Sour	Salty	Bitter	Umami
ice cream	grapefruit	potato chips	coffee	chicken

E Compare your answers in a group. Do you all agree which basic taste each food has? Add some more examples to the chart.

F Check (✓) your favorite foods in the chart. Which of the five basic tastes do you like best? Who in your group shares your sense of taste?

LISTENING

LISTENING 1 | You Are What You Eat

You are going to listen to an excerpt from a radio show in which Andrew Patterson interviews Dr. Maureen O'Ryan, a nutrition expert. As you listen to the excerpt, gather information and ideas about the importance of taste and nutrition.

PREVIEW THE LISTENING

Critical Thinking **Tip**

Activity A asks you to make predictions. When you make predictions, you use what you already know to help you guess the answers.

A. **PREVIEW** Look at this list of foods and drinks. Which do you think have good effects? Which have bad effects? Write *G* (good) or *B* (bad). Then compare your ideas with a classmate. Which of these foods and drinks do you consume most in your diet?

cheese ____   red meat ____

coffee ____   soda ____

dark chocolate ____   tea ____

milk chocolate ____   white meat ____

B. **VOCABULARY** Read aloud these words from Listening 1. Check (✓) the ones you know. Use a dictionary to find the meaning of any words you do not know. Then discuss with a partner how these words may relate to the unit.

balanced *(adj.)*	**mix** *(v.)* 🔑
calories *(n.)*	**mood** *(n.)* 🔑
concentrate *(v.)* 🔑	**rely on** *(phr. v.)*
consume *(v.)*	**spicy** *(adj.)* 🔑
diet *(n.)* 🔑	**wise** *(adj.)* 🔑

🔑 Oxford 3000™ words

 **C.** Go online to listen and practice your pronunciation.

WORK WITH THE LISTENING

A | **LISTEN AND TAKE NOTES** Choose one of the foods or drinks from Activity A in Preview the Listening on page 29. Listen to the interview and take notes on what Dr. O'Ryan says about it. Then tell your partner.

Food or drink: _____

Notes: _____

_____

B. Listen again to the interview. What does Dr. O'Ryan say about each food or drink? Check (✓) the correct answer.

	Better for you	OK in small amounts	Bad for you
1. red meat			
2. white meat			
3. cheese			
4. coffee			
5. tea			
6. soda			
7. milk chocolate			
8. dark chocolate			

C. Read the sentences. Circle the answer that best completes each statement.

1. Dr. O'Ryan's advice is to _____.
   a. eat anything you like
   b. always eat healthy foods
   c. eat a balanced diet

2. Red meat is good for your _____.
   a. eyesight
   b. hair and teeth
   c. bones and skin

3. Eating turkey can help you _____.
   a. feel more relaxed
   b. lose more weight
   c. have better eyesight

4. Cheese can raise your blood pressure because it contains a lot of _____.
   a. oil
   b. salt
   c. calories

5. Too much coffee can _____.
   a. make you feel stressed
   b. give you too much energy
   c. affect your heart

6. Green tea can help you _____.
   a. lose weight
   b. sleep well
   c. concentrate better

7. Calories that have no nutritional value are called _____ calories.
   a. dead
   b. empty
   c. useless

8. Drinking soda can make you feel _____.
   a. happier
   b. more tired
   c. hungrier

9. Dark chocolate _____.
   a. is good for your heart
   b. has less fat than milk chocolate
   c. can increase your blood pressure

D. **Mark these statements *T* (true) or *F* (false). Then write a sentence to explain why, using the information from Listening 1 to support your answers.**

____ 1. It is important to know what effects food and drink have on our bodies.

_____

_____ 2. Eating lots of fruits and vegetables is essential to a healthy diet.

_____

_____ 3. Red meat is just as healthy as white meat.

_____

_____ 4. It is better to avoid drinking coffee.

_____

_____ 5. It is OK to consume things we know are bad for us.

_____

iQ ONLINE **E.** Go online to listen to *Governing What We Eat* and check your comprehension.

F. **VOCABULARY** Use the new vocabulary from Listening 1. Complete each sentence with the correct word from the list.

mix *(v.)*	**rely on** *(phr. v.)*	**calories** *(n.)*	**mood** *(n.)*	**concentrate** *(v.)*
spicy *(adj.)*	**consume** *(v.)*	**diet** *(n.)*	**wise** *(adj.)*	**balanced** *(adj.)*

1. My _____ includes a lot of chicken and rice.

2. If you _____ too much food, you will gain weight.

3. I can't cook, so I _____ my mother to make my meals.

4. I'm not going to eat this candy bar because it has 450 _____.

5. I love chocolate because it always puts me in a good _____.

6. I can't eat _____ food because it upsets my stomach.

7. Do you think it's _____ to go jogging right after a big meal?

8. According to the recipe, you have to _____ the flour and sugar together before adding the eggs.

9. Please don't talk to me while I'm cooking. I need to _____.

10. A good way to stay healthy is to eat _____ meals and exercise regularly.

iQ ONLINE **G.** Go online for more practice with the vocabulary.

SAY WHAT YOU THINK

Discuss the questions in a group.

1. Do you agree with Dr. O'Ryan's advice for a healthy diet? Why or why not?

2. Do you think people worry too much about nutrition? Give examples.

3. Do you agree that "you are what you eat"?

Listening for causes and effects

Speakers often talk about **causes** and **effects** to help explain their opinions. Listening for the linking words and phrases that connect causes (reasons) and effects (results) will help you understand a speaker's main points.

 Here are some words and phrases that signal causes and effects.

I rarely cook **because** I am tired when I get home.
effect — cause

We usually eat at home **since** it's so expensive to eat out these days.
effect — cause

I never buy fish **as** I don't know how to cook it.
effect — cause

The pasta tasted terrible, **so** we didn't eat it.
cause — effect

Due to her healthy diet, Keiko lived to be 110 years old.
cause — effect

Because of the high calories, I never eat chocolate.
cause — effect

Note: Use *due to* and *because of* before noun phrases. Use *because*, *since*, *as*, and *so* before clauses.

A. Listen to the sentences. Complete each sentence with the correct word or phrase.

1. _____ Dr. O'Ryan is a nutrition expert, Andy interviewed her on his radio show.

2. Eating a lot of cheese isn't good _____ the large amount of salt.

3. _____ Andy stopped drinking soda, he feels much healthier now.

4. Andy also wants to lose weight, _____ he's following Dr. O'Ryan's suggestions.

B. Listen to four statements from the radio show. Complete the chart with the causes or effects you hear. Then circle the linking words.

Cause	Effect
1. (Because) it contains a natural substance which makes us feel calm, →	_eating turkey can actually change_ _your mood._
2. Cheese has calcium, →	_____

Effect	Cause
1. Coffee gives you energy ←	_____
2. The calories in soda are what we call "empty" calories ←	_____

C. Think about your diet. How does what you eat affect you? For example, does it make you feel tired or awake, nervous or happy? Does the time of day make a difference? Make notes and share your ideas with a partner. Be sure to use linking words and phrases when giving causes and effects.

I never eat ice cream because it makes my teeth hurt.

Sometimes I drink coffee in the morning as it helps to wake me up.

iQ ONLINE   **D.** Go online for more practice with listening for causes and effects.

Note-taking Skill   Taking notes on causes and effects

When listening to identify causes and effects, you need to listen carefully for the key words and phrases that are used to introduce both causes and their effects.

To introduce a cause, you may hear: *as, because, because of, due to, since*

To introduce an effect, you may hear: *as a result, consequently, so, therefore*

It is also useful to prepare a T-chart to help you classify the information. Write *Cause* and *Effect* in a T-chart and note each piece of information in the appropriate column as you listen. Organizing your notes in this way will help you understand how the ideas relate to one another. It will also make it easier to review your notes.

A. Read this section of a talk on nutrition. Circle the words that introduce causes and effects.

Fast food is more popular today than ever before. Because of our busy lifestyle, people don't always have time to cook their own meals. It may be more expensive than cooking for yourself, but every day millions of us choose a pizza or take-out instead of a home-cooked meal. The downside is that although fast food is quick and easy, it is expensive, so it can be bad for our wallets. What's more, it is bad for our health, too, as a lot of fast food contains high levels of sugar and salt. Also, it is easy to eat too much due to special promotions that encourage us to buy more than we need. For all these reasons, we need to start making healthier food choices.

B. Use this T-chart to complete each cause and effect.

Cause	Effect
1. busy lifestyle	_____ _____
2. it is expensive	_____ _____
3. _____ _____	bad for health
4. _____ _____	eat too much

C. Go online for more practice taking notes on causes and effects.

LISTENING 2 | Food Tasters

UNIT OBJECTIVE
You are going to listen to some lectures from a career website. Three professional food tasters talk about their jobs. As you listen, gather information and ideas about the importance of taste and nutrition.

PREVIEW THE LISTENING

cheese

A. **PREVIEW** What skills do you think a food taster needs to have? Do you think this job requires training? What kinds of foods do you think a food taster might taste?

chocolate

coffee

B. **VOCABULARY** Read aloud these words from Listening 2. Check (✓) the ones you know. Use a dictionary to find the meaning of any words you do not know. Then discuss with a partner how these words may relate to the unit.

complex *(adj.)* 🔑	flavor *(n.)* 🔑	swallow *(v.)* 🔑
disgusting *(adj.)* 🔑	keep an eye on *(phr.)*	texture *(n.)*
distinguish *(v.)* 🔑	occasionally *(adv.)* 🔑	trend *(n.)* 🔑
estimate *(v.)* 🔑		

🔑 Oxford 3000™ words

 **C.** Go online to listen and practice your pronunciation.

WORK WITH THE LISTENING

🔊 **A.** **LISTEN AND TAKE NOTES** Listen to three professional food tasters talk about their jobs. Before you listen, look at the T-charts below. As you listen, complete the causes and effects.

Tip for Success

Remember to listen carefully for key words that introduce causes and effects.

Stuart

Cause	Effect
loves chocolate	this is his _____
everybody _____	volunteers easy to find
easy to put on weight	tries to _____
has to keep up with _____	travels a lot

Marie

Cause	Effect
all taste different	need to _____
keep cheeses for a long time	has to decide _____
need to _____	convenient to live outside Paris
people like to try _____	must develop new products

Enrique

Cause	Effect
sense of taste best in mornings	only _____
people pay a lot for coffee	want to _____
tastes up to 100 coffees	doesn't _____
lives _____	walks to work

B. Read the statements. Listen again to Stuart and Marie and write *T* (true) or *F* (false). Then correct the false statements.

Stuart …

___ 1. has a degree in nutrition.

___ 2. started this job immediately after graduation.

___ 3. visits the dentist once a year.

Marie …

___ 4. doesn't like strong-smelling cheeses.

___ 5. often visits local farmers.

___ 6. has a degree in food science.

C. Listen again to Enrique. Circle the answer that best completes each statement.

1. Enrique started work as a (manager / waiter) in a coffee shop.

2. He (has / does not have) a professional qualification.

3. He works for a large (importing / exporting) company.

4. He checks the (price / quality) of the coffee.

5. In the afternoons he (emails clients / contacts suppliers).

D. Read these summaries. Work with a partner to find two mistakes in each one. Correct the mistakes.

1. Stuart is a chocolate taster for an ice cream manufacturer. He has a degree in nutrition. He trains staff, visits factories, and deals with suppliers. He has worked in his current job for eight years. He likes to keep fit and eat healthily.

2. Marie is a cheese buyer for a large supermarket. On a taste day, she checks the flavor, texture, and smell of up to 10 different cheeses. She especially likes strong-smelling cheeses. She sometimes gets tired of her job.

3. Enrique works as a trainee coffee taster. He checks the quality of coffee, its smell and taste, and how sweet or bitter it is. He loves his job. To him, trying to tell the differences between different coffees is very easy.

In Unit 1 you learned
about suffixes. Review
the common suffixes
on page 17. Notice
how these suffixes
can help you identify
the correct part of
speech.

E. VOCABULARY Use the new vocabulary from Listening 2. Read the sentences. Circle the answer that best matches the meaning of each bold word or phrase.

1. Some of the best dishes are made with a variety of spices. This gives them a **complex** flavor.

   a. complicated　　　b. uninteresting　　　c. important

2. That cheese smells **disgusting**. Throw it away!

   a. disappointing　　　b. amazing　　　c. terrible

3. Hold your nose and close your eyes, and you'll find it hard to **distinguish** between an onion and an apple.

   a. see　　　b. know　　　c. tell the difference

4. Scientists don't exactly know, but they **estimate** that 80 percent of what we taste is due to smell.

   a. promise　　　b. agree completely　　　c. calculate approximately

5. Children often don't like to eat food with strong **flavors**, but they grow to like them as they get older.

   a. senses　　　b. tastes　　　c. feelings

6. Could you **keep an eye on** the cookies in the oven while I'm out? I don't want them to burn.

   a. think about　　　b. listen to　　　c. check often

7. I don't eat eggs much, but **occasionally** I have an omelet.

   a. frequently　　　b. never　　　c. sometimes

8. You should **swallow** your vitamins with a full glass of water.

   a. try　　　b. take　　　c. mix

9. I don't like the **texture** of this bread—it's too hard for me.

   a. feel　　　b. look　　　c. taste

10. I don't take dieting **trends** seriously since they change so often.

   a. fashions　　　b. meals　　　c. restaurants

iQ ONLINE **F.** Go online for more practice with the vocabulary.

SAY WHAT YOU THINK

A. Discuss the questions in a group.

1. Which do you like best: chocolate, cheese, or coffee? Why do you like it so much?

2. Do you think you might like to be a food taster? Why or why not?

B. Before you watch the video, discuss the questions in a group.

1. What kinds of foods contain carbohydrates? Is it better to eat before or after exercise?

2. How can food help the brain? Are some foods better for the brain than others? Does it really matter what time of day you eat?

iQ ONLINE

C. Go online to watch a video about food and the body and brain. Then check your comprehension.

> **VIDEO VOCABULARY**
>
> **carbohydrate** *(n.)* a substance found in sugar that gives your body energy
>
> **glucose** *(n.)* a type of sugar
>
> **protein** *(n.)* a substance found in meat and fish that helps you grow and be healthy
>
> **starchy** *(adj.)* foods like rice and bread that contain a lot of starch
>
> **stock up on** *(phr. v.)* to collect a supply of

D. Think about the unit video, Listening 1, and Listening 2 as you discuss the questions.

1. In what ways can what we eat affect our health and well-being? How healthy is your diet and lifestyle?

2. Who is most responsible for making sure we make the right food choices: the government, parents, teachers, or ourselves? How can people who eat unhealthy food be encouraged to change their habits?

Collocations are combinations of words that are often used together. For example, certain adjectives go together with certain nouns. Using correct collocations will make your conversations sound more natural.

Here are some examples of adjective-noun collocations.

> When you eat before exercising, you should only have a **light meal.**
> There is nothing better than a **cold drink** on a hot summer day.
> I try not to eat too much **fast food**, but it's difficult because I love fries.
> Would you like cheesecake for dessert or just some **fresh fruit**?

A. Complete each collocation with a noun from the box.

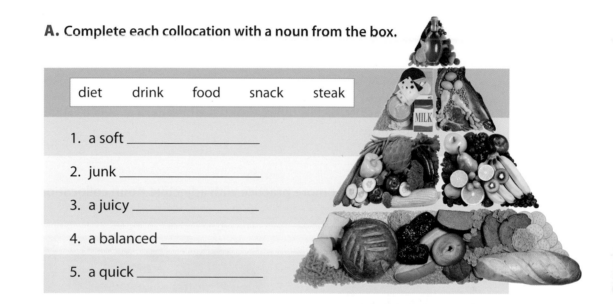

diet	drink	food	snack	steak

1. a soft _____

2. junk _____

3. a juicy _____

4. a balanced _____

5. a quick _____

B. Complete each sentence with the correct collocation from Activity A.

1. Jim's favorite meal to cook at home is _____, served with potatoes.

2. To have _____, you need to eat lots of different kinds of foods.

3. Do you want tea, or would you like _____ with lunch?

4. I used to eat chips and candy all the time. Now I hate _____!

5. I don't have time for a big lunch, so let's just have _____.

C. Circle the answer that best completes each collocation.

1. James has always had a very _____ appetite.
   a. healthy
   b. fit

2. Generally, I try to avoid eating a lot of fatty _____.
   a. cooking
   b. foods

3. Is all the fish on the menu deep _____?
   a. grilled
   b. fried

4. _____ exercise is an important part of staying healthy.
   a. Regular
   b. Steady

5. I like cooking, but I hate washing all the _____ dishes afterwards.
   a. filthy
   b. dirty

iQ ONLINE **D. Go online for more practice with adjective-noun collocations.**

SPEAKING

UNIT
OBJECTIVE

At the end of this unit, you will interview three classmates about their favorite dishes. Make sure to give advice when you conduct your interviews.

Grammar	Quantifiers with count/noncount nouns

Count nouns are the names of things we can count, for example, one egg and two bananas. **Noncount nouns** are the names of things we cannot count, such as cheese and water.

how many/how much

Use *how many* with count nouns. Use *how much* with noncount nouns.

> **How many** apples do you eat a week?
> **How much** tea do you drink a day?

too many/too much

Use *too many/too much* when there is more than you want or need.

> You can have cookies once in a while, but don't eat **too many**.
> Don't drink **too much** coffee at bedtime, or you'll never fall asleep.

enough/not enough

Use *enough/not enough* with both count and noncount nouns.

> We have **enough** food for everybody.
> We don't have **enough** chairs.

A. Complete the conversations with words and phrases from the box. Then practice the conversations with a partner.

enough	many	too many
not enough	much	too much

chilies

Eileen: Hey, that smells great. What are you cooking?

Debra: Chicken with chilies and rice. Do you want to try some?

Eileen: Sure … Wow! That's hot! How _____ chilies did you
                put in?   1

Debra: Five. But they're really small. Don't you like spicy food?

Eileen: Yeah, I do, but it's too hot for me!

Anna: What do you think of the soup? It's potato and onion.

Susie: Hmm. It's OK. It seems like there is something missing, though.

Anna: Maybe I didn't put in _____ salt.
                                              2

Susie: And it's pretty thick, isn't it?

Anna: Yes. I think I used _____ potatoes.
                                              3

Muriel: How _____ sugar did you put in this coffee?
                              4

Angela: One teaspoon.

Muriel: That's _____ for me! I like my coffee very sweet.
                                5

Angela: Well, you shouldn't have _____. You'll get fat.
                                                      6

Tip for Success

When listening, make sure you maintain eye contact. This encourages the speaker and shows that you are interested.

B. Make a list of foods and drinks you like. Write *C* (count) or *N* (noncount) next to each item. Then discuss your favorite things to eat and drink with a partner. Be sure to use *much*, *many*, and *enough* correctly with count and noncount nouns.

Foods I like ...   Drinks I like ...

_____   _____

_____   _____

_____   _____

C. Go online for more practice using quantifiers with count and noncount nouns.

D. Go online for the grammar expansion.

When certain words follow each other, additional sounds are created. These extra sounds make a natural **link** between the two words.

When a word beginning with a vowel follows a word that ends in the vowel sounds /i/, /eɪ/, or /aɪ/ (like *bee, say,* or *eye*), a /j/ sound is added between the words.

> I think Marco must **be** /j/ **Italian.**
> I can't see you tonight, but Tues**day** /j/ **is** fine.
> **I** /j/ **ate** salmon for dinner last night.

When a word beginning with a vowel follows a word that ends in the vowel sounds /u/, /o/, or /aʊ/ (like *who, no* and *how*), a /w/ sound is added between the words.

> Do **you** /w/ **eat** a balanced diet?
> Do you want to **go** /w/ **out** for lunch?
> **How** /w/ **is** your steak?

Pronouncing these linking sounds will help make your English sound more natural.

A. Listen to the sentences. Write /j/ or /w/ in the correct places. Then listen again and check your answers.

1. We /j/ all eat things we know we shouldn't.

2. "Empty" calories have no nutritional value at all.

3. I can't drink coffee, but tea is fine.

4. Cheese has calcium, so it's good for your teeth.

5. Sometimes in the evening I'm too tired to cook.

6. Marie makes sure the cheese is ready to go out on sale.

7. Stuart thinks the appearance of chocolate can be as important as the taste.

8. Enrique thinks people pay a lot for coffee so they want to enjoy it.

B. Listen again. Repeat each sentence. Practice linking /j/ and /w/.

iQ ONLINE **C.** Go online for more practice using links with /j/ and /w/.

The words *should*, *shouldn't*, and *ought to* are used to give advice. Listen to these sentences.

According to Dr. O'Ryan, Andy **should** drink less coffee.
He **shouldn't** drink a lot of soda.
He **ought to** eat more fish.

You can sound more polite by starting a sentence with *perhaps*.

Perhaps you **should** eat more fruit and vegetables.

You can give stronger advice by adding *really*.

You **really ought to** eat more fruit and vegetables.

A. Work with a partner. Discuss your eating and drinking habits. Take turns making true statements about your diet. After each of your partner's statements, give some advice, using *should/shouldn't* or *ought to*. Remember to use count/noncount nouns correctly.

A: *I probably eat too much fast food.*
B: *You should try to eat more healthily. For example, you shouldn't eat fries for lunch. Perhaps you should eat a salad instead.*

B. Think about the advice your partner gave you. Work in a group. Share the advice you received.

I eat too much fast food, so I should try to eat more healthily. For example, I ought to eat a salad for lunch instead of fries.

 **C.** Go online for more practice giving advice.

UNIT
OBJECTIVE ▶▶▶ In this assignment, you are going to interview three classmates about their favorite dishes. As you prepare your interview, think about the Unit Question, "What's more important: taste or nutrition?" Use information from Listening 1, Listening 2, the unit video, and your work in this unit to support your interview. Refer to the Self-Assessment checklist on page 50.

CONSIDER THE IDEAS

Work in a group. Match each dish with the country it comes from. Then discuss which dishes you have tried and whether or not you liked them.

_____ 1. fondue   a. Japan

_____ 2. pizza   b. Saudi Arabia

_____ 3. kabsa   c. Switzerland

_____ 4. moussaka   d. Greece

_____ 5. sushi   e. Mexico

_____ 6. tacos   f. Italy

fondue

What other dishes from around the world do you know? In your group, quiz each other on where different dishes come from.

A: *Where does paella come from?*
B: *Uh … Spain!*

Paella Valenciana

PREPARE AND SPEAK

A. GATHER IDEAS Make a list of your favorite dishes, either from your own country or from other cultures.

_____   _____

_____   _____

_____   _____

B. ORGANIZE IDEAS Choose one dish from your list in Activity A. Use the outline to help you prepare to talk about it. Do not write exactly what you are going to say. Just write notes to help you organize your ideas.

MY **FAVORITE** DISH

What's the name of the dish?

_____

Where is it from? _____

What are the ingredients? _____

_____

How healthy is this dish? _____

Why do you particularly like this dish? _____

_____

_____

_____

Tip for Success

When making notes, don't write full sentences. Just write the important words.

C. SPEAK Complete these steps. Refer to the Self-Assessment checklist on page 50 before you begin.

1. Interview three students.

2. Ask them about their favorite dishes from Activity B, and take notes in the chart.

3. When you talk about your own favorite dish, use your notes from Activity B to help you. Do not read exactly what you wrote; just use your notes.

	Classmate 1	Classmate 2	Classmate 3
Dish			
Country			
Ingredients			
Is it healthy?			
Reasons for liking it?			

4. When you finish, discuss your interviews in a group. Do more of your classmates choose their favorite dish because of taste or nutrition? Whose favorite dish would you like to try?

 Go online for your alternate Unit Assignment.

CHECK AND REFLECT

A. **CHECK** Think about the Unit Assignment as you complete the Self-Assessment checklist.

SELF-ASSESSMENT		
Yes	**No**	
☐	☐	I was able to speak easily about the topic.
☐	☐	My classmates understood me.
☐	☐	I used vocabulary from the unit.
☐	☐	I used quantifiers with count/noncount nouns.
☐	☐	I used links with /j/ and /w/.
☐	☐	I gave advice.

B. **REFLECT** Go to the Online Discussion Board to discuss these questions.

1. What is something new you learned in this unit?

2. Look back at the Unit Question—What's more important: taste or nutrition? Is your answer different now than when you started this unit? If yes, how is it different? Why?

TRACK YOUR SUCCESS

Circle the words and phrases you have learned in this unit.

Nouns
calories
diet 🔑
flavor 🔑
mood 🔑
texture
trend 🔑 AWL

Verbs
concentrate 🔑 AWL
consume AWL
distinguish 🔑
estimate 🔑 AWL

mix 🔑
swallow 🔑

Adjectives
balanced
complex 🔑 AWL
disgusting 🔑
spicy 🔑
wise 🔑

Adverbs
occasionally 🔑
perhaps 🔑
really 🔑

Phrasal Verbs
rely on

Phrases
keep an eye on

Collocations
cold drink
fast food
fresh fruit
light meal

🔑 Oxford 3000™ words
AWL Academic Word List

Check (✓) the skills you learned. If you need more work on a skill, refer to the page(s) in parentheses.

LISTENING ☐	I can listen for causes and effects. (p. 33)
NOTE TAKING ☐	I can take notes on causes and effects (p. 35)
VOCABULARY ☐	I can use adjective-noun collocations. (p. 41)
GRAMMAR ☐	I can use quantifiers with count/noncount nouns. (p. 43)
PRONUNCIATION ☐	I can link words with /j/ and /w/ sounds. (p. 45)
SPEAKING ☐	I can give advice. (p. 46)
UNIT OBJECTIVE ▶▶▶ ☐	I can gather information and ideas to conduct a class survey on food preferences.

UNIT 3

Psychology

NOTE TAKING	▶	taking notes on advantages and disadvantages
LISTENING	▶	listening for time markers
VOCABULARY	▶	using the dictionary
GRAMMAR	▶	tag questions
PRONUNCIATION	▶	intonation in tag questions
SPEAKING	▶	asking for and giving reasons

UNIT QUESTION

Is change good or bad?

A Discuss these questions with your classmates.

1. What has been the biggest change in your life recently? How did it affect you?

2. Is there anything in your life right now that you would like to change?

3. Look at the photo. What kind of change is taking place? Would you ever make this kind of change in your life? How?

B Listen to *The Q Classroom* online. Then answer these questions.

1. Felix thinks that most changes have a good and a bad side. Do you agree? Can you think of any examples?

2. Yuna says she is happy about starting school full time. How did you feel when you began your course here? How did your life change as a result?

iQ ONLINE **C** Go to the Online Discussion Board to discuss the Unit Question with your classmates.

OVERSIZE LOAD

D Complete the questionnaire.

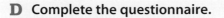

HOW DO YOU FEEL ABOUT **Change?**

1 **When I go on vacation, I prefer to…**

a. go to the same place every year.
b. go somewhere different each time.

2 **When I watch TV, I…**

a. watch the same programs every week.
b. try to find something new to watch.

3 **When I go shopping for food, I usually…**

a. buy the same things.
b. look for something different.

4 **The idea of moving to a different city makes me feel…**

a. worried.
b. excited.

5 **When it's time to have my hair cut, I prefer to…**

a. keep the same hairstyle.
b. try a different look if I feel like it.

6 **In my future career, I think I will…**

a. have the same job my whole life.
b. try a few different jobs.

7 **When it comes to my TV, cell phone, and camera, I usually…**

a. keep them until they break.
b. replace them when I want to.

8 **When I buy new clothes, I usually…**

a. choose the same style and color.
b. look for something in the latest fashion.

How well did you do?

If you chose *a* for most of your answers, you prefer things to stay the same, and perhaps feel fairly cautious about change. You know what you like, so trying new things worries you. Don't be afraid to take a few chances from time to time—you might enjoy something different.

If you chose *b* for most of your answers, you are happy to try new experiences and are open to new ideas. You love variety, but be careful—you don't need to change everything all the time! Perhaps you should think more carefully before you decide to change things.

If you chose *a* and *b* equally, you are very balanced. You welcome change sometimes, but you don't want things to change all the time. Congratulations!

E Discuss your answers in a group. Do you think the questionnaire is accurate? Why or why not? Use examples from your own life to support your opinion.

Using a T-chart is a simple way to separate information when you take notes. You can use a T-chart to help you see two sides of an argument, the advantages and disadvantages of a topic, or the strengths and weaknesses of an idea.

When someone is giving their opinion on a subject, you can use a T-chart to separate their opinions when you take notes. Simply write *Advantages* and *Disadvantages* in a T-chart and note each opinion in the appropriate column as you listen. This will help you understand the opposing viewpoints more clearly.

A. Read this section of a talk on the impact of the Internet. Underline the opinions in favor of and against the Internet.

The Internet has profoundly changed the way we live. Unlike traditional mail, we can communicate instantly with people anywhere in the world. We can keep in touch with family and friends. Companies can promote their products and services 24 hours a day via websites. We can also find information on almost any topic and access a wide range of entertainment; we can play games, watch movies, etc. However, some people say the Internet can harm relationships as it replaces face-to-face communication with a virtual world. Other drawbacks include unwanted emails (spam), viruses, which can damage your computer, and spyware that steals your personal information. Not everyone welcomes the changes that the Internet has brought.

B. Note each advantage and disadvantage in the T-chart.

Critical Thinking **Tip**

In Activity B, you use a T-chart to **summarize** the advantages and disadvantages of the Internet. When you summarize, you give the main points but not all the details.

Advantages	Disadvantages

C. Work with a partner. Discuss the advantages and disadvantages of the Internet. Use your T-chart from Activity B to help you.

iQ ONLINE

D. Go online for more practice taking notes on advantages and disadvantages.

LISTENING 1 | Changing Expectations

You are going to listen to Gary McBride talk about how his life has changed after leaving a high-paying job on Wall Street to work in a small town in Iowa. As you listen to the talk, gather information and ideas about the advantages and disadvantages of change.

PREVIEW THE LISTENING

Gary McBride

A. PREVIEW Why do you think Gary wanted to do something different? Check (✓) your predictions.

☐ He was bored with his job.

☐ He wanted to travel around the world.

☐ He decided to start his own business.

☐ He wanted to spend more time with his family.

B. VOCABULARY Read aloud these words from Listening 1. Check (✓) the ones you know. Use a dictionary to define any new or unknown words. Then discuss with a partner how the words will relate to Gary's story.

adapt *(v.)* 🔑	**handle** *(v.)* 🔑
considerably *(adv.)* 🔑	**justify** *(v.)* 🔑
crisis *(n.)* 🔑	**position** *(n.)* 🔑
curious *(adj.)* 🔑	**steady** *(adj.)* 🔑
fulfilled *(adj.)*	**suffer** *(v.)* 🔑

🔑 Oxford 3000™ words

  C. Go online to listen and practice your pronunciation.

WORK WITH THE LISTENING

A. **LISTEN AND TAKE NOTES** Listen to an excerpt from Gary's talk. He is talking about his life as a city trader. As you listen, take notes in the T-chart on the advantages and disadvantages he mentions.

Tip for Success

Using a **T-chart** is a simple way to separate information when you take notes.

Life as a city trader	
Advantages	**Disadvantages**
very well paid	

B. Now listen to another excerpt from Gary's talk. Here, he is talking about his life as a home-care assistant. As you listen, take notes in the T-chart on the advantages and disadvantages he mentions.

Life as a home-care assistant	
Advantages	**Disadvantages**

C. Read the questions. Then listen again to the whole talk. Circle the best answer for each question.

1. Why did Gary stop working as a city trader?
   a. He lost his job.
   b. He became ill.
   c. He couldn't handle the stress.

2. What did Gary do as soon as he left his job?
   a. He looked for another job.
   b. He traveled.
   c. He moved back home.

3. Why did Gary move to Iowa?
   a. He wanted to be near his parents.
   b. He needed to find a better job.
   c. He had some good friends there.

4. How does Gary feel about his new job?
   a. It's very fulfilling.
   b. It can be difficult.
   c. The salary is too low.

5. What goal has Gary achieved?
   a. He has more time to think.
   b. He is happy.
   c. He enjoys his free time.

D. Read these statements. Write *T* (true) or *F* (false). Then correct the false statements.

____ 1. According to Gary, many people consider "downshifting" at some point in their lives.

_____

____ 2. After finishing work as a city trader, he decided to retrain before looking for a new career.

_____

____ 3. He was unemployed for six months.

_____

____ 4. He rejected several job offers before starting work again.

_____

____ 5. These days he feels he is a better person.

_____

 E. Go online to listen to *Change and Stress* and check your comprehension.

F. VOCABULARY Use the new vocabulary from Listening 1. Read the sentences. Then match each bold word with its definition below.

____ 1. When the economic **crisis** started, people were suddenly worried about losing their jobs.

____ 2. Tina couldn't **handle** all the noise and pollution of living in a city, so she moved to the country.

____ 3. When Brian left his small village to live in the city, it took him a few months to **adapt**.

____ 4. We're **curious** about what it would be like to live in another country. It sounds very interesting.

____ 5. Over the years, Steve's company has developed **steady** and reliable relationships with many other businesses in the area.

____ 6. I felt **fulfilled** as a teacher because I enjoyed helping people learn.

____ 7. There were more than 30 applications for the **position** of general manager.

____ 8. Don't you agree that keeping things the same is **considerably** easier than trying to change them?

____ 9. After I borrowed money from my parents, I had to **justify** the purchases I made with it.

____ 10. If you focus too much on your job, your personal relationships may **suffer** as a result.

a. *(v.)* to change your behavior because the situation you are in has changed
b. *(adv.)* a lot
c. *(n.)* a time of great danger or difficulty
d. *(adj.)* wanting to know or learn something
e. *(adj.)* completely satisfied and happy
f. *(v.)* to control or deal with someone or something
g. *(v.)* to give or be a good reason for something
h. *(n.)* a job
i. *(adj.)* staying the same over a period of time
j. *(v.)* to become worse in quality

iQ ONLINE | **G.** Go online for more practice with the vocabulary.

SAY WHAT YOU THINK

Discuss the questions in a group.

1. What did Gary learn by changing his career? Do you think the lesson will last?

2. What benefits from his old job might Gary miss?

3. Do you think you could change your life completely in this way? Why or why not?

When listening to a narrative, such as someone telling a story, it can be useful to listen for time markers. Time markers help to establish when something happened, for how long, etc. By listening for time markers, you can more easily understand past events and how they relate to one another. Here are some words and phrases that are commonly used as time markers.

> now/nowadays
> before/after
> then, next, after that
> three days **ago**
> **for** two weeks
> these days

A. Listen again to Gary's talk. Match each time marker (a–e) with an event (1–5).

a. A few years ago

b. Then

c. For six months

d. After a couple of months

e. These days

1. the financial crisis came along.

2. I'm still a home-care assistant.

3. I started looking for work.

4. I worked on Wall Street.

5. I traveled around the world.

B. Think about an important change that happened in your life. Make notes, using time markers to help clarify what happened and when.

C. Work with a partner. Discuss the important change in your life, using the notes you made in Activity B. Make sure you use time markers to help your partner understand.

iQ ONLINE **D.** Go online for more practice listening for time markers.

You are going to listen to a radio interview with Barbara Ehrenreich, a well-known journalist and author. As you listen to the interview, gather information and ideas about the advantages and disadvantages of change.

PREVIEW THE LISTENING

Barbara Ehrenreich

A. PREVIEW Why do you think a journalist might decide to "go undercover" to do research? Discuss your ideas with a partner.

B. VOCABULARY Read aloud these words from Listening 2. Check (✓) the ones you know. Use a dictionary to define any new or unknown words. Then discuss with a partner how the words will relate to the unit.

cope (v.) 🔑	research (n.) 🔑
exhausted (adj.)	struggle (v.) 🔑
firsthand (adv.)	support (oneself) (v.) 🔑
informed (adj.)	unemployed (adj.) 🔑
permanent (adj.) 🔑	wages (n.) 🔑

🔑 Oxford 3000™ words

 **C.** Go online to listen and practice your pronunciation.

WORK WITH THE LISTENING

A. LISTEN AND TAKE NOTES Listen to the first part of the interview with Barbara Ehrenreich. As you listen, take notes on her reasons for going undercover.

Reasons for going undercover

need to experience something _____

a good way to _____

can write about experiences from a more _____

B. Read the statements. Then listen to the second part of the interview. Write *T* (true) or *F* (false). Correct the false statements.

____ **1.** For *Nickel and Dimed*, Ehrenreich took several low-paying jobs.

_____

___ 2. Ehrenreich found that it wasn't so difficult to cope financially.

_____

___ 3. For *Bait and Switch*, Ehrenreich researched unemployment among white-collar workers.

_____

___ 4. Ehrenreich found that life was more difficult for white-collar workers than unskilled workers.

_____

___ 5. Ehrenreich is pleased that the changes she made were temporary.

_____

___ 6. Ehrenreich didn't learn as much as she expected by going undercover.

_____

C. Read the statements. Then listen again. Circle the answer that best completes each statement.

1. For her book *Nickel and Dimed*, Ehrenreich worked undercover in each job for _____.
   a. one month
   b. three months
   c. six months

2. While Ehrenreich was working undercover, _____.
   a. she studied hard
   b. she had a lot of fun
   c. her life changed completely

3. Ehrenreich found that it was difficult to manage financially because _____ were so high.
   a. food prices
   b. travel expenses
   c. rents

4. Ehrenreich says that some of the jobs made her feel _____.
   a. very tired
   b. very bored
   c. very angry

5. Ehrenreich didn't expect *Nickel and Dimed* to be so _____.
   a. expensive
   b. popular
   c. easy to write

6. For her next book, *Bait and Switch*, Ehrenreich _____.
   a. used a false name
   b. took several top jobs
   c. didn't do any research

7. For *Bait and Switch*, Ehrenreich pretended to be an unemployed _____ executive.
   a. account
   b. human resources
   c. public relations

8. Even though Ehrenreich claimed to have _____, she couldn't find any work.
   a. letters of recommendation
   b. a lot of experience
   c. great qualifications

D. Work with a partner. Take notes on each book. In what ways are they similar? In what ways are they different?

Book	Notes
Nickel and Dimed	
Bait and Switch	

Vocabulary Skill Review

In Unit 2, you learned about adjective-noun collocations. Can you find any adjective-noun collocations in Activity E? Underline them.

E. **VOCABULARY** Use the new vocabulary from Listening 2. Read the sentences. Circle the answer that best matches the meaning of each bold word or phrase.

1. It can be very difficult for people working in low-paying jobs to **cope**.
   a. manage financially
   b. build relationships
   c. be happy

2. After working for ten hours without a break, we were **exhausted**.
   a. very excited
   b. very bored
   c. very tired

3. It's hard to truly understand someone else's situation. Sometimes you need to experience it **firsthand**.
   a. quickly
   b. directly
   c. together

4. You need to know all the facts before you can make an **informed** decision.
   a. detailed
   b. serious
   c. educated

5. Agostino is always happy. He has a **permanent** smile on his face.
   a. constant
   b. occasional
   c. attractive

6. Sociologists are doing **research** on how people live in the poorest parts of the city.
   a. estimates
   b. practice
   c. studies

7. Many people who don't have jobs **struggle** when it is time to pay their bills.
   a. work hard
   b. have difficulty
   c. invest money

8. Many students at college don't receive money from their parents. They need to be able to **support themselves**.
   a. take care of themselves
   b. live together
   c. enjoy themselves

9. When the company closed down, many of its workers became **unemployed**.
   a. jobless
   b. educated
   c. sick

10. I enjoy my work, but the **wages** are too low for me to make a living.
    a. benefits
    b. earnings
    c. conditions

SAY WHAT YOU THINK

A. Discuss the questions in a group.

1. Why do you think *Nickel and Dimed* was a best seller?

2. What qualities do you think a person needs to go undercover as Ehrenreich did? Would you like to try doing this? Why or why not?

 for Success

Be an active listener! Use expressions such as *Really?*, *Hmm, Yeah,* and *I see* to show that you are paying attention to the speaker.

B. Before you watch the video, discuss these questions in a group.

1. How easy do you think it is for someone to change careers?

2. What are the challenges in changing to a completely different kind of job? What are the potential benefits?

iQ ONLINE

C. Go online to watch a video about how Christine Marchuska changed her life after losing her job on Wall Street. Then check your comprehension.

---

burned-out *(adj.)* feeling as if you have done something too long and need a rest

ecstatic *(adj.)* very happy, excited, and enthusiastic

head back *(v.)* return

Ivy League *(n.)* a group of eight universities in the United States with high academic standards, a prestigious social status, and long-standing traditions

philanthropy *(n.)* the practice of helping the poor and those in need

VIDEO VOCABULARY

D. Think about the unit video, Listening 1, and Listening 2 as you discuss these questions.

1. Think about the changes that Gary McBride and Barbara Ehrenreich experienced. How were their experiences similar? How were they different?

2. What did each person learn from change? Who do you think learned more? Explain your reasons.

A **word web** is a diagram that connects words. You can use a word web to show the different meanings of a word.

- Start with a word with multiple meanings, such as *get*. Write the word in the middle circle of the word web.
- Next, look up the word in the dictionary. Some dictionaries have shortcuts, words that help you find the different meanings more quickly.
- Write each shortcut word in a circle surrounding the middle circle.
- Include an example sentence to help you understand the word and show how it is used in English.

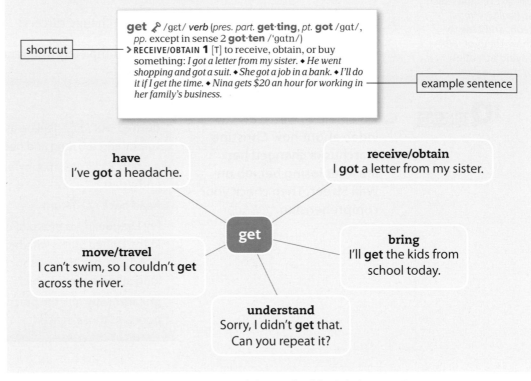

All dictionary entries are from the *Oxford American Dictionary for learners of English* © Oxford University Press 2011.

A. Read the sentences. Then write the number of each sentence below the correct shortcut in the word web. Use a dictionary to help you if necessary.

1. This town has changed a lot in recent years.

2. You need to change the light bulb in the kitchen.

3. It's quicker by bus, but you have to change twice.

4. Do you want to change before we go out?

5. Can you change a twenty-dollar bill?

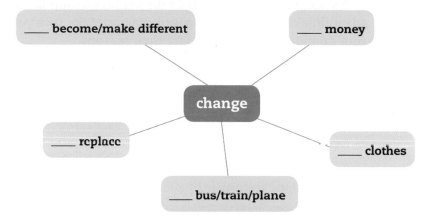

_____ become/make different

_____ money

change

_____ replace

_____ clothes

_____ bus/train/plane

B. Work with a partner. Use a dictionary to help you complete this word web with the verb *make*. Follow the steps in the Vocabulary Skill box.

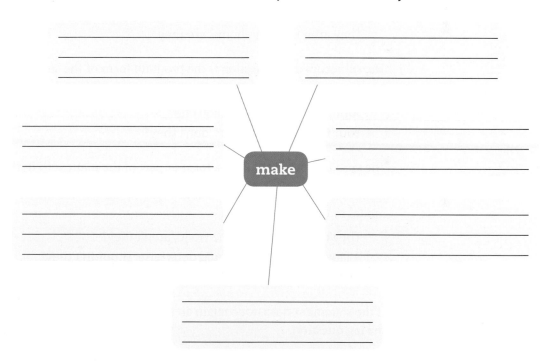

make

iQ ONLINE **C.** Go online for more practice with using the dictionary.

SPEAKING

At the end of this unit, you will take part in a group discussion about the advantages and disadvantages of change. Make sure you give reasons for your opinions and ask others for their reasons.

Grammar | Tag questions

Tag questions are common in everyday conversation. You can use a tag question to keep a conversation going by asking a person for her opinion about a situation.

Tag questions are formed by adding a short *yes/no* question at the end of a statement.

If the statement is positive, the tag question is negative.

> Starting a new job **is** exciting, **isn't it**?

If the statement is negative, the tag question is positive.

> They **aren't** moving home, **are they**?

The subject of a tag question is the pronoun form of the subject of the statement.

> **You**'re starting your own business, aren't **you**?
> **John** went to Australia, didn't **he**?
> **Your friends** all have jobs, don't **they**?

The verb in a tag question is a form or part of the main verb in the statement.

If the statement contains an auxiliary verb or modal, use the auxiliary verb or modal in the tag question.

> They**'re** curious about the world, **aren't** they?
> All low-paid workers **should** get a raise, **shouldn't** they?
> You **haven't** told anyone you're leaving, **have** you?

If the statement does not contain an auxiliary verb or modal, use a form of *do* in the tag question.

> Your boss **trusts** you, **doesn't** he?
> The crisis **got** better, **didn't** it?

A. Use tag questions to complete the conversations. Then practice the conversations with a partner.

1. A: You're a journalist, _____?

   B: Yes, I am.

2. A: Simon never works on the weekend, _____?

B: No, he doesn't.

3. A: They got married, _____?

B: No, they didn't.

4. A: It's important to have good friends, _____?

B: Yes, it is.

5. A: Susan should see her family more often, _____?

B: Yes, she should.

6. A: Abed and Gary don't have permanent jobs, _____?

B: No, they don't.

7. A: Valerie came here from France, _____?

B: Yes, she did.

8. A: We can't afford an overseas vacation this year, _____?

B: Yes, we can!

B. **Complete the sentences. Use tag questions. Then add three more sentences with tag questions of your own.**

1. You don't like to get your hair cut, _____?

2. You haven't bought a new cell phone, _____?

3. You're not thinking of moving abroad, _____?

4. _____?

5. _____?

6. _____?

C. **Work with a partner. Take turns asking and answering the questions from activity B.**

iQ ONLINE **D.** **Go online for more practice with tag questions.**

E. **Go online for the grammar expansion.**

The **intonation** you use in tag questions is very important. Use falling intonation on the tag question when you think you know the answer and you are asking for confirmation. Use rising intonation on the tag question when you are not certain of the answer.

Asking for confirmation

Carol's never worked abroad, has she?   You can scuba dive, can't you?

Uncertain of the answer

Carol's never worked abroad, has she?   You can scuba dive, can't you?

A. Listen to the sentences. Does the intonation rise or fall on each tag question? Check (✓) your answers.

		Rise	Fall
1.	You've never been to Europe, have you?	☐	☐
2.	Julie and Frank just had a baby, didn't they?	☐	☐
3.	You're not looking for a new job, are you?	☐	☐
4.	James is retiring next year, isn't he?	☐	☐
5.	Kieron moved to New York last year, didn't he?	☐	☐
6.	The new housing project was approved, wasn't it?	☐	☐

B. Listen to the sentences. Does the speaker know the answer or not? Check (✓) your answers.

		Knows the answer	Doesn't know the answer
1.	You've tried horseback riding, haven't you?	☐	☐
2.	Adapting to a new job can be hard, can't it?	☐	☐
3.	You wouldn't like to live in New York, would you?	☐	☐
4.	You're not afraid of change, are you?	☐	☐
5.	Travel is exciting, isn't it?	☐	☐
6.	You don't want to work for yourself, do you?	☐	☐

C. Listen again to the sentences from Activities A and B. Repeat the sentences. Use the same intonation that you hear.

D. Work with a partner. Take turns reading the sentences from Activities A and B. Your partner will listen carefully and decide whether your intonation rises or falls.

 E. Go online for more practice with intonation in tag questions.

Speaking Skill	Asking for and giving reasons

To better understand someone's point of view, you can ask the person to explain the **reasons** for his or her opinion. You can also help people understand your point of view by explaining your own reasons. Here are some phrases you can use to ask for or give reasons.

Asking for reasons
Why do you think/say that?
What are your reasons for saying that?
Can you explain why …?

Giving reasons
because …
because of/due to …
The reason … is (that) …
That's why …

To give several reasons for your point of view, you can introduce each reason with a phrase like these.

First (of all),
Also/Second,
Another reason/thing is …
Finally,

Listen to how the phrases are used in this conversation.

A: You know, I really don't think fishing is for me.
B: Oh yeah? **Why do you say that?**
A: Well, **first of all**, it's boring! **Also**, it's expensive to buy all the equipment, and **another thing** I hate is the smell of fish!

A. Listen to a conversation between two friends. Complete the conversation with the phrases you hear. Then practice the conversation with a partner.

Tip for Success

A good way to keep a conversation going is to ask questions. Asking for more information often helps a conversation become more interesting, too.

Jez: I haven't seen you for ages. How was your vacation in Spain?

Tom: It was great! I tried lots of new things—horseback riding, scuba diving … I even went to a bullfight in Madrid.

Jez: What? You went to a bullfight? I'm surprised.

Tom: Really? _____ ?
₁

Jez: _____ it's cruel, isn't it? Why would you
2

want to watch that?

Tom: Well, _____ , it's an important part of the
3

culture … you know? _____ it's really popular.
4

Lots of tourists were there. It's _____ good to
5

experience something different for a change … I think.

B. Work in a group. Look at the activities in the box. Discuss which activities
you would like to try. Give reasons for your ideas.

white-water rafting

bungee jumping	shopping	white-water rafting
gardening	surfing	rock-climbing
other: _____		

A: _I'd like to try white-water rafting. That sounds amazing._

B: _Really? Why do you say that? I think it sounds scary._

A: _Well, first of all, I love water sports, and another reason is
that it looks very exciting._

iQ ONLINE   **C.** Go online for more practice asking for and giving reasons.

Unit Assignment   Take part in a group discussion

UNIT
OBJECTIVE ▶▶▶▶

In this assignment, you are going to take part in a group discussion about
the advantages and disadvantages of change. As you prepare for the group
discussion, think about the Unit Question, "Is change good or bad?" Use
information from Listening 1, Listening 2, the unit video, and your work in this
unit to support your discussion. Refer to the Self-Assessment checklist on page 74.

CONSIDER THE IDEAS

Work in a group. Think about the following important events that can occur
in people's lives. Each event represents a big change. Discuss the advantages
and disadvantages that each event might have. Use phrases from the
Speaking Skill box on page 71 to practice giving and asking for reasons.

changing your job	passing an exam
getting married	starting at a new school/college
studying abroad	

PREPARE AND SPEAK

A. **GATHER IDEAS** Think about the events you discussed with your group. Choose one of the events that you have experienced yourself. Then write answers to the questions.

Which event did you choose? _____

Did you experience the advantages and disadvantages you discussed with your group? What were they?

_____

_____

_____

_____

_____

What did you learn from this event?

_____

_____

_____

B. **ORGANIZE IDEAS** Complete the outline. Use ideas from your discussion and your notes from Activity A. Think about change in general as you answer the questions. Do not write exactly what you are going to say. Just write notes to help you organize your ideas.

What are the advantages of change?

_____

_____

_____

_____

What are the disadvantages of change?

_____

_____

_____

What can we learn from change?

_____

_____

_____

Tip for Success

When listening to your classmates, take notes of the main points each person makes. You can use these notes later when you want to ask questions.

C. SPEAK Discuss your ideas in a group. Do not read exactly what you wrote. Just use your notes. Use phrases from the Speaking Skill box on page 71 to give and ask for reasons. Decide who in your group has a view of change similar to your own. Refer to the Self-Assessment checklist below before you begin.

 Go online for your alternate Unit Assignment.

CHECK AND REFLECT

A. CHECK Think about the Unit Assignment as you complete the Self-Assessment checklist.

SELF-ASSESSMENT		
Yes	No	
☐	☐	I was able to speak easily about the topic.
☐	☐	My group understood me.
☐	☐	I used vocabulary from the unit.
☐	☐	I used tag questions.
☐	☐	I used intonation in tag questions.
☐	☐	I asked for reasons for someone's opinion and gave reasons for my own opinions.

B. REFLECT Go to the Online Discussion Board to discuss these questions.

1. What is something new you learned in this unit?

2. Look back at the Unit Question—Is change good or bad? Is your answer different now than when you started this unit? If yes, how is it different? Why?

TRACK YOUR SUCCESS

Circle the words and phrases you have learned in this unit.

Nouns
crisis 🔑
position 🔑
research 🔑 **AWL**
wages 🔑

Verbs
adapt 🔑 **AWL**
change 🔑
cope 🔑
get 🔑
handle 🔑
justify 🔑 **AWL**
struggle 🔑
suffer 🔑
support (oneself) 🔑

Adjectives
curious 🔑
exhausted
fulfilled
informed
permanent 🔑
steady 🔑
unemployed 🔑

Adverbs
Also, 🔑
considerably 🔑 **AWL**
Finally, 🔑 **AWL**
First, 🔑
firsthand
Second, 🔑

Phrases
Another reason/thing
   is …
Can you explain why …?
First of all,
That's why …
The reason … is (that) …
What are your reasons
   for saying that?
Why do you think/say
   that?

🔑 Oxford 3000™ words
AWL Academic Word List

Check (✓) the skills you learned. If you need more work on a skill, refer to the page(s) in parentheses.

NOTE TAKING ☐	I can use a chart to take notes on advantages and disadvantages. (p. 55)
LISTENING ☐	I can listen for time markers. (p. 60)
VOCABULARY ☐	I can use word webs. (p. 66)
GRAMMAR ☐	I can use tag questions. (p. 68)
PRONUNCIATION ☐	I can use intonation in tag questions. (p. 70)
SPEAKING ☐	I can ask for and give reasons. (p. 71)
UNIT OBJECTIVE ▶▶▶ ☐	I can gather information and ideas to participate in a group discussion about change.

UNIT **4**		
	LISTENING ▶	identifying fact and opinion
	VOCABULARY ▶	context clues to identify meaning
	GRAMMAR ▶	modals expressing attitude
	PRONUNCIATION ▶	intonation in questions
	SPEAKING ▶	giving and supporting your opinions
Marketing	NOTE TAKING ▶	using a mind map to note opinions

UNIT QUESTION

How can advertisers change our behavior?

A Discuss these questions with your classmates.

1. When you watch television, do you usually watch the commercials? What television ads can you think of right now?

2. How often do you click on Internet ads? Do you buy things on the Internet?

3. Look at the photos. What kinds of advertisements do you see?

🔊 **B** **Listen to *The Q Classroom* online. Then answer these questions.**

1. Marcus thinks that advertising makes a product seem more familiar to us, and as a result we are more likely to buy it. Do you agree? Did you ever buy something because you saw an ad?

2. Felix says that advertising helps companies become more famous, and people tend to trust famous companies more than companies they don't know. Do you agree? Which companies do you trust?

 **C** **Go online to watch a video about innovative marketing. Then check your comprehension.**

consensus *(n.)* an opinion that all members of a group agree with

open the floodgates *(phr.)* start something that will be difficult to stop

put up *(phr. v.)* installed

subliminally *(adv.)* affecting your mind even though you are not aware of it

VIDEO VOCABULARY

 **D** **Go to the Online Discussion Board to discuss the Unit Question with your classmates.**

E Complete the questionnaire.

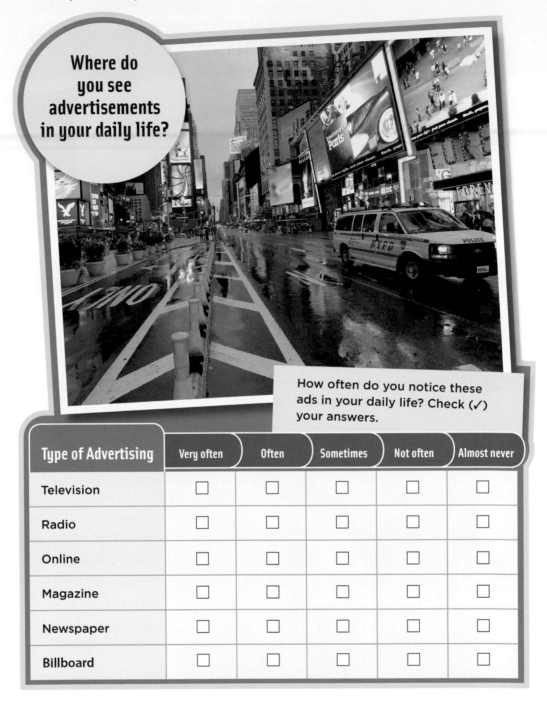

Where do you see advertisements in your daily life?

How often do you notice these ads in your daily life? Check (✓) your answers.

Type of Advertising	Very often	Often	Sometimes	Not often	Almost never
Television	☐	☐	☐	☐	☐
Radio	☐	☐	☐	☐	☐
Online	☐	☐	☐	☐	☐
Magazine	☐	☐	☐	☐	☐
Newspaper	☐	☐	☐	☐	☐
Billboard	☐	☐	☐	☐	☐

F Compare your answers with a partner. What are the advantages and disadvantages of each type of advertising? Which types do you pay most attention to?

LISTENING

LISTENING 1 | Advertising Techniques

 **UNIT OBJECTIVE** You are going to listen to a group of students giving a presentation. As you listen to the presentation, gather information and ideas about how advertisers can change our behavior.

PREVIEW THE LISTENING

A class was given an assignment to research advertising on local radio. One group of students is presenting their ideas to the class, explaining various advertising techniques used in the ads they heard.

A. **PREVIEW** What kinds of products do you expect to hear advertised on the radio? Think of five products and write them down. Then share your ideas with the class.

B. **VOCABULARY** Read aloud these words from Listening 1. Check (✓) the ones you know. Use a dictionary to define any new or unknown words. Then discuss with a partner how the words will relate to the unit.

appeal *(n.)* 🔑	**logo** *(n.)*
brand *(n.)* 🔑	**memorable** *(adj.)*
campaign *(n.)* 🔑	**persuade** *(v.)* 🔑
claim *(v.)* 🔑	**relate to** *(phr.)* 🔑

🔑 Oxford 3000™ words

iQ **ONLINE** **C.** Go online to listen and practice your pronunciation.

WORK WITH THE LISTENING

🔊 **A.** **LISTEN AND TAKE NOTES** Look at the advertising techniques in the chart. Listen to the students give their presentation. Take notes on each advertising technique they mention.

Advertising technique	Notes
Emotional appeal	
Association of ideas	
Bandwagon	
Repetition	
Humor	

B. Use your notes to match each ad with a technique from the chart.

Name of ad

1. Dan's Diner _e_

2. Seattle Security ___

3. Robertson's Black ___

4. Perfect Pens ___

5. Arizona Market ___

Now match the descriptions in the box to the techniques in the chart. Compare your ideas with a partner. Then listen again and check your answers.

Technique	Description of technique
a. Emotional appeal	
b. Humor	
c. Bandwagon	g
d. Association of ideas	
e. Repetition	

> f. links the product with positive ideas
> g. claims the product is very popular
> h. focuses on feelings and emotions
> i. gives key information over and over again
> j. makes people laugh

C. Read the statements. Write T (true) or F (false). Correct the false statements.

___ 1. There is no charge for a security assessment from Seattle Security.

___ 2. Seattle Security specializes in fitting high-quality alarms.

___ 3. Robertson's Black is a chocolate bar made in Switzerland.

___ 4. Arizona Market is a family event that takes place next Saturday.

___ 5. Arizona Market starts at noon.

___ 6. The special offer at Dan's Diner is available all week.

___ 7. There is no charge for teenagers at Dan's Diner.

___ 8. There are three varieties of Perfect Pens.

D. With a partner, decide which advertising technique to use with each of these products. Take notes of your reasons. Then make a group and explain your ideas.

1. A baby stroller	2. A fragrance for men	3. A cell phone

iQ ONLINE **E.** Go online to listen to *Marketing Social Change* and check your comprehension.

F. **VOCABULARY** Use the new vocabulary from Listening 1. Read the sentences. Circle the answer that best matches the meaning of each word or phrase in bold.

Tip for Success

Keep a small notebook with you for new words and phrases. Check your notes when you get home.

1. I don't like negative advertising. I can't understand its **appeal**.
   a. attraction   b. title   c. product

2. This **brand** of toothpaste is the best one on the market.
   a. design   b. management   c. kind

3. The ad **campaign** was expensive, but it didn't produce great results.
   a. promotion   b. sample   c. poster

4. Many ads **claim** that their products have fantastic benefits, but don't give any proof.
   a. imagine   b. state   c. suppose

5. Everyone wore T-shirts showing the company's new **logo** of a jumping tiger.
   a. product   b. design   c. example

6. That company won the award for the most **memorable** ad of the year. People were still talking about it months afterwards.
   a. current   b. unforgettable   c. exciting

7. Advertisers use several techniques to **persuade** consumers to buy certain products.

   a. support   b. instruct   c. convince

8. Ads often try to **relate to** us on an emotional level.

   a. reply to   b. connect with   c. help

 G. Go online for more practice with the vocabulary.

SAY WHAT YOU THINK

Discuss the questions in a group.

1. Which radio ads in Listening 1 do you like most? Why?

2. Which advertising technique do you think is the most effective? Explain your reasons.

3. Think of an ad you have seen or heard recently. What product was it advertising? Which technique did it use? How effective do you think it was?

Listening Skill Identifying fact and opinion

When you listen, it is important to identify what is a **fact** and what is someone's **opinion**.

A fact is something that is always true and can be proved.

⌈ Paris is the capital of France.
⌊ Soccer matches last 90 minutes.

An opinion is something that cannot be proved. People might disagree about an opinion.

⌈ Paris is the most beautiful city in the world.
⌊ Soccer is a great game for young children.

 A. Listen to these statements from the radio ads you heard in Listening 1. Decide whether each statement is a fact or an opinion. Circle your answers.

1. fact / opinion

2. fact / opinion

3. fact / opinion

Tip for Success

The next time you listen to the radio, focus on the ads. Listen carefully, and try to identify what is fact and what is opinion.

B. Now listen to statements from another ad describing a personal computer. Decide whether each statement is a fact or an opinion. Circle your answers.

1. fact / opinion

2. fact / opinion

3. fact / opinion

4. fact / opinion

5. fact / opinion

6. fact / opinion

iQ ONLINE | **C.** Go online for more practice identifying fact and opinion.

LISTENING 2 | Advertising Ethics and Standards

UNIT OBJECTIVE ▶▶▶▶ You are going to listen to an interview with Mary Engle, associate director for advertising practices at the U.S. Federal Trade Commission (FTC). As you listen to the interview, gather information and ideas about how advertisers can change our behavior.

PREVIEW THE LISTENING

The Federal Trade Commission is an independent agency of the U.S. government. It is responsible for keeping American business competition free and fair. Mary Engle directs the Division of Advertising Practices. The Division is responsible for regulating national advertising matters, including claims about food, OTC (over the counter) drugs, dietary supplements, and Internet services.

A. PREVIEW Mary Engle explains some of the ways in which advertising is controlled. In what ways do you think companies that break the advertising rules can be punished? Make a list of your ideas, and then compare with a partner.

B. VOCABULARY Read aloud these words from Listening 2. Check (✓) the ones you know. Use a dictionary to define any new or unknown words. Then discuss with a partner how the words will relate to the unit.

aimed at *(phr.)* 🔑	mislead *(v.)*
competitor *(n.)*	monitor *(v.)* 🔑
deliberately *(adv.)* 🔑	refund *(n.)*
evidence *(n.)* 🔑	regulations *(n.)* 🔑
injury *(n.)* 🔑	withdraw *(v.)* 🔑

🔑 Oxford 3000™ words

 iQ ONLINE **C.** Go online to listen and practice your pronunciation.

WORK WITH THE LISTENING

A. LISTEN AND TAKE NOTES Listen to the interview and take notes in the chart.

1. How the FTC finds ads that break the rules	
2. Examples of ways advertisers can be punished	

B. Read the statements. Write *T* (true) or *F* (false) according to what Mary Engle says. Correct the false statements.

_____ 1. The FTC makes sure ads don't break the law.

_____

_____ 2. Today there are fewer controls on advertising than in the past.

_____

_____ 3. The FTC focuses mainly on health advertising.

_____

_____ 4. Advertisers follow different regulations, depending on where the ad appears (for example, TV or radio).

_____

_____ 5. The FTC only checks ads on TV and radio.

_____

_____ 6. The FTC can take various steps to stop advertisers that break the rules.

_____

_____ 7. Monitoring advertising today is more difficult than in the past.

_____

_____ 8. The way companies advertise has not changed much over the years.

_____

C. Read the sentences. Then listen again. Circle the answer that best completes each statement.

1. The "truth-in-advertising" laws mean that advertisers shouldn't _____.
    a. advertise to children
    b. mislead the public
    c. make claims without providing evidence

2. As an example of untruthful advertising in the past, Engle mentions _____.
    a. weight loss products
    b. beauty products
    c. health food products

3. Engle says the main aim of the FTC is to make sure advertisers _____.
    a. don't overcharge people
    b. act responsibly
    c. don't criticize other companies

4. The FTC doesn't allow ads that might cause people to suffer physical or _____ harm.
    a. emotional
    b. personal
    c. financial

5. The FTC can only regulate _____ advertising.
    a. national
    b. state
    c. local

6. Engle gives an example of a fast food chain that broke the rules because
    _____.
    a. it claimed its food was healthy
    b. its food was too expensive
    c. its food made people ill

7. The FTC punished the fast food chain by _____.
    a. telling the company to withdraw the ad
    b. closing the company
    c. fining the company

8. Deliberately putting a funny video on the Internet that features a product
    is called _____.
    a. sub-viral marketing
    b. product placement
    c. Web promotion

**Vocabulary
Skill Review**

In Unit 3, you learned
that many words
have more than one
meaning. Use your
dictionary to find any
different meanings
for each word, and
make notes in your
vocabulary notebook.

D. **VOCABULARY** **Use the new vocabulary from Listening 2. Complete each
sentence with the correct word from the list.**

aimed at (phr.)	**mislead** (v.)
competitor (n.)	**monitor** (v.)
deliberately (adv.)	**refund** (n.)
evidence (n.)	**regulations** (n.)
injury (n.)	**withdraw** (v.)

1. The product didn't work, so the company had to give customers a(n)
    _____.

2. Advertisers may be given heavy fines if they _____
    the public.

3. Ads for games are usually _____ children.

4. If a product causes _____ to customers, then the fines can
    be very large.

5. Sometimes companies have to _____ their products from
    the market because of faults.

6. It's important to _____ ads to check they are fair.

7. Unfortunately, our main _____ has a very good ad campaign at the moment.

8. The company claims that this ad resulted in more sales, but there isn't any _____ of that.

9. Companies that _____ give false information should pay a fine.

10. In the United States, each state decides its own advertising _____.

 E. Go online for more practice with the vocabulary.

SAY WHAT YOU THINK

A. Discuss the questions in a group.

1. Do you think product placement is a successful form of advertising? Explain your opinion. What product placement ads have you seen?

2. Which groups in society do you think are easy for advertisers to influence (children, teenagers, men, or women, for example)? Should advertising regulations be made stronger to protect these groups?

B. Think about the unit video, Listening 1, and Listening 2 as you discuss the questions.

1. What claims do advertisers make to influence people to buy their products (for example, "it's cheap," "it's healthy," etc.)? Make a list of examples from ads in this unit and from other ads you know.

Critical Thinking Tip

Question 2 of Activity B asks you to **evaluate** how truthful certain ad claims are. When you evaluate, you put your knowledge and opinions together.

2. Look at the claims you listed above. What products are likely to make these claims? Name one product for each claim and say whether that claim is usually truthful or not.

When you hear a word or phrase you don't know, it is sometimes possible to determine the meaning from the **context**. Try to identify the part of speech, and think about the words that surround it. Use this information to help you figure out what the word means.

⌐ This magazine has a **circulation** of 100,000 a month.

Circulation is a noun. You can tell it refers to the number of copies of the magazine sold per month.

⌐ We advertise a lot in video games because teenagers are our main **target**.

Target is a noun. You can tell it refers to the type of people that the ad is aimed at.

⌐ **Infomercials** can mislead people into thinking they are watching
└ a TV program.

Infomercial is the subject of the sentence and therefore a noun. You can see that it includes parts of two words you know: **info**rmation and com**mercial**. The context tells you that it refers to a type of TV program: an infomercial is a long commercial advertising a product.

A. Read the sentences. Underline the context clues that help you determine the meaning of each bold word. Compare your ideas with a partner.

1. That ad is <u>so big</u> and <u>colorful</u>. It's very **eye-catching**.

2. That radio station plays the same ads all day. It's **tedious** to hear them over and over.

3. Commercials in **prime time** are the most expensive because the largest number of people watch TV then.

4. We really need a more aggressive marketing strategy to **push** this product if we want it to sell more.

5. The ads for that new book are everywhere, but you shouldn't believe the **hype**. I read it, and it's terrible.

6. The slogan was so **catchy** I couldn't stop thinking about it for days.

B. Write each word from Activity A next to its correct definition. Compare your answers with your partner.

1. _____ : to make something especially noticeable or attractive, so people will buy it

2. _____ : interesting or attractive to look at

3. _____ : the most popular time to watch TV

4. _____ : advertising that makes something seem better than it is

5. _____ : easy to remember

6. _____ : boring and lasting a long time

Over 1000 Products

Fantastic Health Foods

Your Neighborhood Health Food Store

Vitamins
Minerals
Body Care
Books

FAST DELIVERY • BIG SELECTION • HELPFUL STAFF

877-555-2345

 **C.** Go online for more practice using context clues to identify meaning.

SPEAKING

UNIT OBJECTIVE ▶▶▶▶ At the end of this unit, you will take part in a group discussion about how advertisers change our behavior. Make sure to give and support your opinions when you participate in the discussion.

Grammar	Modals expressing attitude

Modal verbs are special *auxiliary verbs* that help to express the attitude of the speaker. They are followed by the base form of the verb.

Prohibition: They **must not** mislead anyone.

They **can't** say anything false.

Strong obligation: Ads **have to** be truthful.

Ads **must** tell the truth.

Recommendation: You **should** tell the FTC if an ad is misleading.

You **shouldn't** believe everything you hear.

There's another ad for that new restaurant. We **ought to** try it.

No obligation: Advertisers **don't have to** send ads for approval.

Note: **Must/must not** are more common in writing than in conversation.

🔊 **A. Listen to the conversation. Circle the modal verbs you hear. Then practice the conversation with a partner.**

Yvonne: Oh, look at that ad. Those poor animals! How can they show them suffering like that? I think it's terrible!

Maureen: Really? I think it's quite effective. They're trying to get your attention, you know.

Yvonne: Well, they (<u>don't have to / can't</u>) do it that way! It's not necessary,
1
and it's upsetting.

Maureen: You (<u>must not / don't have to</u>) look at it if you don't want to.
2

Yvonne: That's not the point. That kind of advertising makes me really angry. I'm sure there's a law that says they (<u>don't have to / can't</u>) use animals
3
like that.

Maureen: Maybe you (<u>should / have to</u>) complain, then.

4

Yvonne: Yes, I think I will. They (<u>shouldn't / don't have to</u>) be allowed to

5

do that!

B. Discuss these questions in a group. Use modals to express your attitude when possible.

1. What do you think about ads that might make people angry?

2. Are there any types of advertising that should not be allowed?

iQ ONLINE **C.** Go online for more practice using modals to express attitude.

D. Go online for the grammar expansion.

Pronunciation | ***Part 1*** **Intonation in questions**

Intonation is different for ***yes/no*** **questions** than it is for ***wh-*** **questions** (questions that begin with *who, what, when, where, why, which,* or *how*). The intonation rises at the end of *yes/no* questions. It falls at the end of *wh-* questions.

Here are some examples from the interview with Mary Engle.

Yes/no **questions**

    Is there an advertising standards code?

    Are the rules the same in other countries?

Wh- **questions**

    How do you find ads that break the rules?

    What areas do you focus on in particular?

A. Listen to the questions. Does the intonation rise or fall at the end? Circle your answers.

1. Do you spend a lot of money on advertising?   rise / fall

2. What do you think of that ad?   rise / fall

3. Is that ad misleading?   rise / fall

4. Does it have a special offer?   rise / fall

5. Why is there so much hype these days?   rise / fall

B. Listen again. Repeat the questions. Use the same intonation that you hear.

Pronunciation | *Part 2* Intonation in questions

Statements as questions

Sometimes a statement is spoken with rising intonation to make it a question. This often happens if the speaker is surprised by what he has just heard.

Listen to how the intonation changes these statements into questions.

Statements

There are no federal regulations.

They're going to withdraw the product.

Questions

There are no federal regulations?

They're going to withdraw the product?

C. Listen to the sentences. Are they spoken as statements or questions? Circle the correct answer and complete each sentence with a period or question mark.

1. There are no federal regulations __?__   statement / (question)

2. The company is giving a refund to all its customers ____   statement / question

3. You're going to withdraw the product ____   statement / question

4. That ad is really annoying ____   statement / question

5. There used to be no controls ____   statement / question

6. The rules aren't the same in other countries ____   statement / question

7. Viral marketing is becoming more popular ____   statement / question

D. Listen again. Then practice with a partner. Take turns saying different sentences from Activity C and deciding whether each sentence is a statement or a question.

iQ ONLINE **E. Go online for more practice with intonation in questions.**

Speaking Skill | Giving and supporting your opinions

It is often useful to support your opinion by giving reasons and examples. Here are some phrases you can use when you want to give your opinion.

Giving opinions

I (don't) think (that)
In my opinion/view,
If you ask me,
As far as I'm concerned,

Here are some phrases you can use to support your opinion.

Supporting opinions

because/as
For example,
For instance,
To give you an example,

In my opinion, there's too much advertising on TV these days. **To give you an example**, a program I watched last night had ads almost every ten minutes! **If you ask me**, they shouldn't show ads in the middle of programs on TV.

A. Listen to this conversation about an ad. Complete the conversation with the phrases that you hear. Then practice the conversation with a partner.

Hugo: Hey. Look at this ad. It's got six famous people in it!

Peter: So what? _____, they should spend less on these
₁
expensive ads and lower the price of their clothes.

Hugo: Hmm. But I like seeing famous people in ads _____ it
₂
makes it kind of cool.

Peter: _____, there are better ways to advertise things.
₃
_____, they could have some facts and statistics or
₄
something. You know, some information …

Hugo: But it's an ad, right? _____, an ad should get people's
₅
attention, and using famous people does that.

Peter: Well, I guess it's eye-catching, but I'm not sure how effective it is.

B. Work with a partner. What do you think of ads that feature famous people? Are they effective? Discuss these questions. Use phrases from the Speaking Skill box to give and support your opinions.

iQ ONLINE **C. Go online for more practice giving and supporting your opinions.**

Note-taking Skill | **Using a mind map to note opinions**

When discussing a topic, it can be useful to use a mind map. This is especially beneficial if you need to take notes on several different opinions. Using a mind map allows you to organize opinions and link supporting details to each opinion in a way that is easy to refer to later.

To make a mind map, first write the topic in the center and draw a circle around it. Then note all the different opinions by drawing a separate line for each opinion outward from the circle. You can add any supporting facts and details next to or below each opinion, as shown in the mind map below.

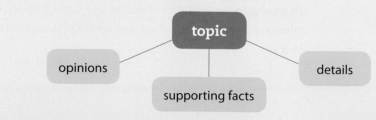

A. Study this mind map of a discussion on celebrity advertising. Notice how the opinions are noted separately along with their supporting ideas.

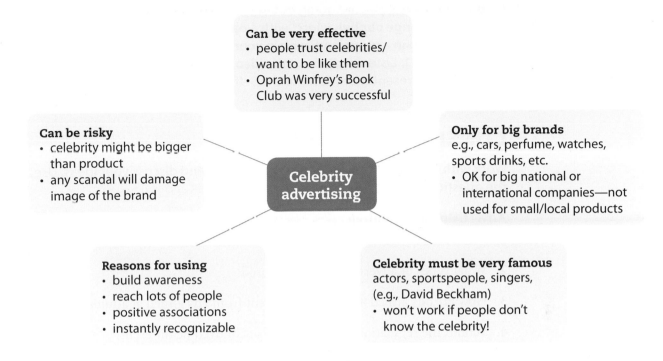

Can be very effective
- people trust celebrities/ want to be like them
- Oprah Winfrey's Book Club was very successful

Can be risky
- celebrity might be bigger than product
- any scandal will damage image of the brand

Celebrity advertising

Only for big brands
e.g., cars, perfume, watches, sports drinks, etc.
- OK for big national or international companies—not used for small/local products

Reasons for using
- build awareness
- reach lots of people
- positive associations
- instantly recognizable

Celebrity must be very famous
actors, sportspeople, singers, (e.g., David Beckham)
- won't work if people don't know the celebrity!

B. Discuss the topic of celebrity advertising using the mind map in Activity A to help you. Add any additional opinions and supporting details.

C. Fill in the mind map below to prepare for a discussion on what makes an advertisement effective. Write your opinions and supporting details in the empty circles. Then discuss your opinions with a partner.

What makes an advertisement effective?

 D. Go online for more practice using a mind map to note opinions.

 | Listening and Speaking   95

UNIT
OBJECTIVE ▶▶▶▶ In this assignment, you are going to discuss the Unit Question, "How can advertisers change our behavior?" with a partner. Then you will summarize your discussion in a group and explain your own opinion. Use information from Listening 1, Listening 2, the unit video, and your work in this unit to support your presentation. Refer to the Self-Assessment checklist on page 98.

CONSIDER THE IDEAS

Work with a partner. Choose one of these topics and discuss your ideas. Use the questions to help you.

Advertising and children

1. What kinds of products are advertised to children?

2. What types of advertising are often used?

3. How are ads aimed at children different from ads aimed at adults?

4. Should the regulations for ads aimed at children be different?

5. Should advertising to children be banned?

Health ads

1. What kinds of health products are advertised?

2. What kind of person is influenced by health ads?

3. Are you influenced by health ads?

4. Should the regulations for health ads be stricter than they are for other ads?

5. Should the advertising of unhealthy products be banned?

Status

1. What kinds of products are advertised as "high class"?

2. Who do you think is the target for these kinds of status ads?

3. Are the claims made by status ads misleading?

4. Why are so many people influenced by this type of advertising?

5. Are you influenced by this type of advertising?

PREPARE AND SPEAK

A. `GATHER IDEAS` Write the topic you chose in the Consider the Ideas activity in the center of the mind map. Then note your answers to each question (1–5) in the space provided. If necessary, add more lines to help you note any additional ideas or opinions.

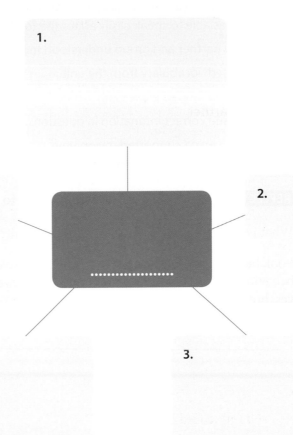

B. `ORGANIZE IDEAS` Support your opinions by adding facts and details. Make notes next to or below each opinion to explain your reasons.

C. `SPEAK` Have a group discussion about how advertisers can influence our behavior. Refer to the Self-Assessment checklist on page 98 before you begin.

1. Take turns presenting your ideas from Activity B.

2. You can refer to your notes, but do not read exactly what you wrote.

3. Give each student a turn as group leader.

 Go online for your alternate Unit Assignment.

CHECK AND REFLECT

A. **CHECK** Think about the Unit Assignment as you complete the Self-Assessment checklist.

Yes	No	SELF-ASSESSMENT
☐	☐	I was able to speak easily about the topic.
☐	☐	My partner and group understood me.
☐	☐	I used vocabulary from the unit.
☐	☐	I used modals expressing attitude.
☐	☐	I used correct intonation in questions.
☐	☐	I gave and supported my opinion.

B. **REFLECT** Go to the Online Discussion Board to discuss these questions.

1. What is something new you learned in this unit?

2. Look back at the Unit Question — How can advertisers change our behavior? Is your answer different now than when you started this unit? If yes, how is it different? Why?

TRACK YOUR SUCCESS

Circle the words and phrases you have learned in this unit.

Nouns
appeal 🔑
brand 🔑
campaign 🔑
circulation
competitor
evidence 🔑 AWL
hype
infomercial
injury 🔑 AWL
logo
refund
regulations 🔑 AWL
slogan
target 🔑 AWL

Verbs
claim 🔑
mislead
monitor 🔑 AWL
persuade 🔑
push 🔑
withdraw 🔑

Adjectives
catchy
eye-catching
memorable
tedious

Adverbs
deliberately 🔑

Phrases
aimed at 🔑
As far as I'm concerned,
because/as
For example,
For instance,
I (don't) think (that)
If you ask me,
In my opinion,
In my view,
prime time
relate to 🔑
To give you an example,

🔑 Oxford 3000™ words
AWL Academic Word List

Check (✓) the skills you learned. If you need more work on a skill, refer to the page(s) in parentheses.

LISTENING	■	I can identify fact and opinion. (p. 82)
VOCABULARY	■	I can identify meaning from context. (p. 88)
GRAMMAR	■	I can use modals to express attitude. (p. 90)
PRONUNCIATION	■	I can use correct intonation in questions. (pp. 91–92)
SPEAKING	■	I can give and support my opinions. (p. 93)
NOTE TAKING	■	I can use a mind map to note opinions. (p. 94)
UNIT OBJECTIVE ▶▶▶	■	I can gather information and ideas to state and support my opinions in a group discussion on advertising.

AUDIO TRACK LIST

Audio can be found in the *iQ Online* Media Center. Go to iQOnlinePractice.com. Click on the Media Center ⊙. Choose to stream or download ⬇ the audio file you select. Not all audio files are available for download.

Page	Track Name: Q2e_03_LS_
2	U01_Q_Classroom.mp3
7	U01_Listening1_ActivityA.mp3
8	U01_Listening1_ActivityD.mp3
11	U01_ListeningSkill_Example.mp3
11	U01_ListeningSkill_ActivityA.mp3
11	U01_ListeningSkill_ActivityC.mp3
12	U01_Listening2_ActivityA.mp3
13	U01_Listening2_ActivityD.mp3
21	U01_Pronunciation_Examples.mp3
21	U01_Pronunciation_ActivityA.mp3
22	U01_SpeakingSkill_Examples.mp3
27	U02_Q_Classroom.mp3
30	U02_Listening1_ActivityA.mp3
30	U02_Listening1_ActivityB.mp3
33	U02_ListeningSkill_Examples.mp3
34	U02_ListeningSkill_ActivityA.mp3
34	U02_ListeningSkill_ActivityB.mp3
37	U02_Listening2_ActivityA.mp3
38	U02_Listening2_ActivityB.mp3
38	U02_Listening2_ActivityC.mp3
45	U02_Pronunciation_Examples.mp3
45	U02_Pronunciation_ActivityA.mp3
45	U02_Pronunciation_ActivityB.mp3
46	U02_SpeakingSkill_Examples.mp3
52	U03_Q_Classroom.mp3
57	U03_Listening1_ActivityA.mp3
57	U03_Listening1_ActivityB.mp3
57	U03_Listening1_ActivityC.mp3
60	U03_ListeningSkill_ActivityA.mp3
61	U03_Listening2_ActivityA.mp3
61	U03_Listening2_ActivityB.mp3
62	U03_Listening2_ActivityC.mp3
70	U03_Pronunciation_Examples.mp3
70	U03_Pronunciation_ActivityA.mp3
70	U03_Pronunciation_ActivityB.mp3
70	U03_Pronunciation_ActivityC.mp3
71	U03_SpeakingSkill_Examples.mp3
71	U03_SpeakingSkill_ActivityA.mp3
77	U04_Q_Classroom.mp3
79	U04_Listening1_ActivityA.mp3
80	U04_Listening1_ActivityB.mp3
82	U04_ListeningSkill_ActivityA.mp3
83	U04_ListeningSkill_ActivityB.mp3
84	U04_Listening2_ActivityA.mp3
85	U04_Listening2_ActivityC.mp3
90	U04_Grammar_ActivityA.mp3

Page	Track Name: Q2e_03_LS_
91	U04_Pronunciation_Part1_Examples.mp3
92	U04_Pronunciation_Part1_ActivityA.mp3
92	U04_Pronunciation_Part1_ActivityB.mp3
92	U04_Pronunciation_Part2_Examples.mp3
92	U04_Pronunciation_Part2_ActivityC.mp3
93	U04_Pronunciation_Part2_ActivityD.mp3
94	U04_SpeakingSkill_ActivityA.mp3
100	U05_Q_Classroom.mp3
105	U05_Listening1_ActivityA.mp3
107	U05_Listening1_ActivityD.mp3
109	U05_ListeningSkill_Part1_Example1.mp3
109	U05_ListeningSkill_Part1_Example2.mp3
109	U05_ListeningSkill_Part1_Example3.mp3
110	U05_ListeningSkill_Part1_ActivityA.mp3
110	U05_ListeningSkill_Part2_Examples.mp3
111	U05_ListeningSkill_Part2_ActivityC.mp3
111	U05_ListeningSkill_Part2_ActivityD.mp3
112	U05_Listening2_ActivityA.mp3
112	U05_Listening2_ActivityD.mp3
119	U05_Pronunciation_Examples.mp3
119	U05_Pronunciation_ActivityA.mp3
120	U05_Pronunciation_ActivityB.mp3
121	U05_SpeakingSkill_ActivityA.mp3
122	U05_UnitAssignment.mp3
127	U06_Q_Classroom.mp3
130	U06_Listening1_ActivityA.mp3
131	U06_Listening1_ActivityC.mp3
133	U06_ListeningSkill_Examples.mp3
133	U06_ListeningSkill_ActivityA.mp3
133	U06_ListeningSkill_ActivityB.mp3
134	U06_Listening2_ActivityA.mp3
135	U06_Listening2_ActivityC.mp3
141	U06_Pronunciation_Examples.mp3
141	U06_Pronunciation_ActivityA.mp3
141	U06_Pronunciation_ActivityB.mp3
141	U06_Pronunciation_ActivityC.mp3
141	U06_Pronunciation_ActivityD.mp3
143	U06_SpeakingSkill_ActivityA.mp3
145	U06_NoteTakingSkill_ActivityC.mp3
150	U07_Q_Classroom.mp3
153	U07_Listening1_ActivityA.mp3
154	U07_Listening1_ActivityC.mp3
157	U07_ListeningSkill_Examples.mp3
158	U07_ListeningSkill_ActivityA.mp3
160	U07_Listening2_ActivityA.mp3
161	U07_Listening2_ActivityB.mp3

Page	Track Name: Q2e_03_LS_
167	U07_Pronunciation_ActivityA.mp3
168	U07_Pronunciation_ActivityB.mp3
168	U07_SpeakingSkill_ActivityA.mp3
175	U08_Q_Classroom.mp3
178	U08_Listening1_ActivityA.mp3
178	U08_Listening1_ActivityC.mp3
181	U08_ListeningSkill_ActivityA.mp3
181	U08_ListeningSkill_ActivityB.mp3
183	U08_Listening2_ActivityA.mp3
184	U08_Listening2_ActivityB.mp3
189	U08_Pronunciation_Example1.mp3
189	U08_Pronunciation_Example2.mp3
189	U08_Pronunciation_ActivityA.mp3
189	U08_Pronunciation_ActivityB.mp3
190	U08_Pronunciation_ActivityD.mp3
190	U08_SpeakingSkill_ActivityA.mp3

Authors

Miles Craven has worked in English language education since 1988, teaching in private language schools, British Council centers, and universities in Italy, Portugal, Spain, Hong Kong, Japan, and the U.K. He has a wide range of experience as a teacher, teacher trainer, examiner, course designer, and textbook writer. Miles is author or co-author of over 30 textbooks, and regularly presents at conferences around the world. He also acts as Advisor for Executive Education programs at the Møller Centre for Continuing Education Ltd., Churchill College, University of Cambridge. His research focuses on helping students develop the skills and strategies they need to become confident communicators. He currently specializes in exam preparation for the TOEIC test.

Kristin Donnalley Sherman holds an M. Ed. in TESL from the University of North Carolina, Charlotte. She has taught ESL/EFL at Central Piedmont Community College in Charlotte, North Carolina for more than fifteen years, and has taught a variety of subjects, including grammar, reading, composition, listening, and speaking. She has written student books, teacher's editions, and workbooks in the area of academic ESL/EFL. In addition, she regularly presents at conferences and workshops internationally.

Series Consultants

ONLINE INTEGRATION

Chantal Hemmi holds an Ed.D. TEFL and is a Japan-based teacher trainer and curriculum designer. Since leaving her position as Academic Director of the British Council in Tokyo, she has been teaching at the Center for Language Education and Research at Sophia University on an EAP/CLIL program offered for undergraduates. She delivers lectures and teacher trainings throughout Japan, Indonesia, and Malaysia.

COMMUNICATIVE GRAMMAR

Nancy Schoenfeld holds an M.A. in TESOL from Biola University in La Mirada, California, and has been an English language instructor since 2000. She has taught ESL in California and Hawaii, and EFL in Thailand and Kuwait. She has also trained teachers in the United States and Indonesia. Her interests include teaching vocabulary, extensive reading, and student motivation. She is currently an English Language Instructor at Kuwait University.

WRITING

Marguerite Ann Snow holds a Ph.D. in Applied Linguistics from UCLA. She teaches in the TESOL M.A. program in the Charter College of Education at California State University, Los Angeles. She was a Fulbright scholar in Hong Kong and Cyprus. In 2006, she received the President's Distinguished Professor award at Cal State, LA. She has trained EFL teachers in Algeria, Argentina, Brazil, Egypt, Libya, Morocco, Pakistan, Peru, Spain, and Turkey. She is the author/editor of publications in the areas of integrated content, English for academic purposes, and standards for English teaching and learning. She recently served as a co-editor of *Teaching English as a Second or Foreign Language* (4th ed.).

VOCABULARY

Cheryl Boyd Zimmerman is a Professor at California State University, Fullerton. She specializes in second-language vocabulary acquisition, an area in which she is widely published. She teaches graduate courses on second-language acquisition, culture, vocabulary, and the fundamentals of TESOL and is a frequent invited speaker on topics related to vocabulary teaching and learning. She is the author of *Word Knowledge: A Vocabulary Teacher's Handbook* and Series Director of *Inside Reading, Inside Writing,* and *Inside Listening and Speaking,* all published by Oxford University Press.

ASSESSMENT

Lawrence J. Zwier holds an M.A. in TESL from the University of Minnesota. He is currently the Associate Director for Curriculum Development at the English Language Center at Michigan State University in East Lansing. He has taught ESL/EFL in the United States, Saudi Arabia, Malaysia, Japan, and Singapore.

HOW TO USE iQ ONLINE

iQ ONLINE extends your learning beyond the classroom. This online content is specifically designed for you! *iQ Online* gives you flexible access to essential content.

Activities include
- Additional **practice** and support
- **Videos**—watch anytime, anywhere
- **Online tests** assigned by your teacher.

Progress reports show what skills you have learned and where you still need more practice.

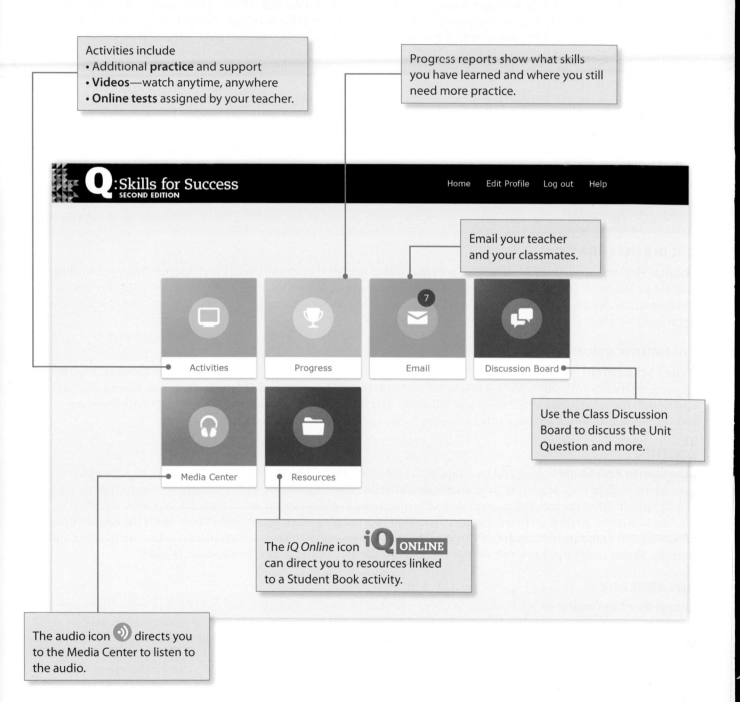

Q:Skills for Success
SECOND EDITION

Home   Edit Profile   Log out   Help

Email your teacher and your classmates.

Activities   Progress   Email   Discussion Board

Media Center   Resources

Use the Class Discussion Board to discuss the Unit Question and more.

The *iQ Online* icon **iQ ONLINE** can direct you to resources linked to a Student Book activity.

The audio icon directs you to the Media Center to listen to the audio.

SEE THE INSIDE FRONT COVER FOR HOW TO REGISTER FOR *iQ ONLINE* FOR THE FIRST TIME.

Take Control of Your Learning

You have the choice of where and how you complete the activities. Access your activities and view your progress at any time.

Your teacher may

- assign *iQ Online* as homework,
- do the activities with you in class, or
- let you complete the activities at a pace that is right for you.

iQ Online makes it easy to access everything you need.

Set Clear Goals

STEP 1 If it is your first time, look through the site. See what learning opportunities are available.

STEP 2 The Student Book provides the framework and purpose for each online activity. Before going online, notice the goal of the exercises you are going to do.

STEP 3 Stay on top of your work, following the teacher's instructions.

STEP 4 Use *iQ Online* for review. You can use the materials any time. It is easy for you to do follow-up activities when you have missed a class or want to review.

Manage Your Progress

The activities in *iQ Online* are designed for you to work independently. You can become a confident learner by monitoring your progress and reviewing the activities at your own pace. You may already be used to working online, but if you are not, go to your teacher for guidance.

Check 'View Reports' to monitor your progress. The reports let you track your own progress at a glance. Think about your own performance and set new goals that are right for you, following the teacher's instructions.

iQ Online is a research-based solution specifically designed for English language learners that extends learning beyond the classroom. I hope these steps help you make the most of this essential content.

C. n. Hemm

Chantal Hemmi, EdD TEFL
Center for Language Education and Research
Sophia University, Japan

Note-taking Skill | Taking notes with examples

When discussing a topic, you may want to give examples to help support your opinion. Taking notes with examples is therefore a very useful skill. It allows you to organize your ideas and support your opinions in a way that is easy to refer to when you are speaking.

Look at these main points and examples from Listening 1. Notice how the main points are noted separately, next to the supporting examples.

Main points	Examples
1. Make sure your goals are realistic.	short, 30-year-old male smoker shouldn't quit job to become basketball player
2. Aiming for success should not cause stress or anxiety.	no example
3. Success can bring problems.	• famous people (TV presenters and sports stars, etc.) who have relationship problems • a high school friend, successful businessman but is now divorced

A. Think of different examples to support each main point in the chart below. Then discuss the topic of success with a partner.

Main points	Examples
1. Make sure your goals are realistic.	
2. Aiming for success should not cause stress or anxiety.	
3. Success can bring problems.	

iQ ONLINE **B.** Go online for more practice taking notes with examples.

192 | UNIT 8 | What can we learn from success and failure?

Notice the icon. It directs you to the online materials linked to the Student Book activities.

Q: Skills for Success
SECOND EDITION   Home   Edit Profile   Log out   Help

Mariel Zuarino   My achievements   My grades

1 Sociology
★★★ 🏆   Excellent! You got 100% of all the points in the unit.

2 Nutritional Science
★★★ 🏆   Well done! You got over 90% of all the points in the unit.

3 Informational Technology
★★☆ 🏆   You got over 70% of all the points in the unit.

Grammar
average score   completed 23 of 44
76%

Vocabulary
average score   completed 12 of 72
100%

Tests
average score   completed 46 of 63
92%

🔑 The keywords of the **Oxford 3000**™ have been carefully selected by a group of language experts and experienced teachers as the words which should receive priority in vocabulary study because of their importance and usefulness.

AWL **The Academic Word List** is the most principled and widely accepted list of academic words. Averil Coxhead gathered information from academic materials across the academic disciplines to create this word list.

The Common European Framework of Reference for Languages (CEFR) provides a basic description of what language learners have to do to use language effectively. The system contains 6 reference levels: **A1, A2, B1, B2, C1, C2**. CEFR leveling provided by the Word Family Framework, created by Richard West and published by the British Council. http://www.learnenglish.org.uk/wff/

UNIT 1

assume (v.) 🔑 AWL , A1
behavior (n.) 🔑, A1
briefly (adv.) 🔑, B1
conscious (adj.) 🔑, A2
effective (adj.) 🔑, A1
encounter (n.) 🔑 AWL , B1
error (n.) 🔑 AWL , A2
expert (n.) 🔑 AWL , A2
negative (adj.) 🔑 AWL , A2
positive (adj.) 🔑 AWL , A2
sample (n.) 🔑, A2
select (v.) 🔑 AWL , A2
suspicious (adj.) 🔑, B1

UNIT 2

complex (adj.) 🔑 AWL , A2
concentrate (v.) 🔑 AWL , A2
consume (v.) AWL , B1
diet (n.) 🔑, A2
disgusting (adj.) 🔑, B1
distinguish (v.) 🔑, B1
estimate (v.) 🔑 AWL , A2
flavor (n.) 🔑, B1
occasionally (adv.) 🔑, B1
mix (v.) 🔑, A2
mood (n.) 🔑, B1
spicy (adj.) 🔑, B1
swallow (v.) 🔑, B1
trend (n.) 🔑 AWL , A2
wise (adj.) 🔑, B1

UNIT 3

adapt (v.) 🔑 AWL , B1
considerably (adv.) 🔑, B2
cope (v.) 🔑, B1
crisis (n.) 🔑, A2
curious (adj.) 🔑, B1
handle (v.) 🔑, A2
justify (v.) 🔑, B1
permanent (adj.) 🔑, A2
position (n.) 🔑, B1
research (n.) 🔑 AWL , A2
steady (adj.) 🔑, B1
struggle (v.) 🔑, A2
suffer (v.) 🔑, A1
support (v.) 🔑, B2
unemployed (adj.) 🔑, B1
wages (n.) 🔑, A2

UNIT 4

aimed at (phr.) 🔑, B1
appeal (n.) 🔑, A2
brand (n.) 🔑, B1
campaign (n.) 🔑, A2
claim (v.) 🔑, A1
deliberately (adv.) 🔑, B1
evidence (n.) 🔑 AWL , A1
injury (n.) 🔑 AWL , A2
monitor (v.) 🔑 AWL , B1
persuade (v.) 🔑, A2
regulations (n.) 🔑 AWL , A2
relate to (phr.) 🔑, A1
withdraw (v.) 🔑, A1

UNIT 5

audience (n.) 🔑, A1
discover (v.) 🔑, A1
embarrass (v.) 🔑, B2
expose (v.) 🔑 AWL , B1
financial (adj.) 🔑 AWL , A1
funds (n.) 🔑 AWL , A1
income (n.) 🔑 AWL , A1
invention (n.) 🔑, B2
investigate (v.) 🔑 AWL , A2
locate (v.) 🔑 AWL , B1
model (n.) 🔑, A2
mystery (n.) 🔑, B1
previous (adj.) 🔑 AWL , A1
promote (v.) 🔑 AWL , B1
prove (v.) 🔑, A1
publish (v.) 🔑 AWL , A1
reputation (n.) 🔑, B1
retire (v.) 🔑, B1
solve (v.) 🔑, A2
threaten (v.) 🔑, A1

UNIT 6

appropriate (adj.) 🔑 AWL , A1
benefit (n.) 🔑 AWL , A1
consumer (n.) 🔑 AWL , A1
demand (v.) 🔑, B1
fair (adj.) 🔑, A2
guilty (adj.) 🔑, A2
ignore (v.) 🔑 AWL , A1
impact (n.) 🔑 AWL , B1
influence (v.) 🔑, A2
lie (v.) 🔑, A1

profit (n.) 🔑, A1
sensible (adj.) 🔑, B1
trust (v.) 🔑, A2

UNIT 7

acquire (v.) 🔑 AWL , A2
analysis (n.) 🔑 AWL , A1
associated with (adj.) 🔑, B2
circumstances (n.) 🔑 AWL , A2
complicated (adj.) 🔑, B1
conduct (v.) 🔑 AWL , A2
demonstrate (v.) 🔑 AWL , A2
dramatic (adj.) 🔑 AWL , B1
immediate (adj.) 🔑, A2
independence (n.) 🔑, A2
outcome (n.) AWL , A2
pleasure (n.) 🔑, A2
somewhat (adv.) 🔑 AWL , A2

UNIT 8

achieve (v.) 🔑 AWL , A1
determination (n.) 🔑, B1
develop (v.) 🔑, B1
emphasize (v.) 🔑 AWL , A2
fear (v.) 🔑, A2
goal (n.) 🔑 AWL , A2
lack (v.) 🔑, B1
measure (v.) 🔑, A1
permit (v.) 🔑, A2
preparation (n.) 🔑, A2
realistic (adj.) 🔑, B2
ruin (v.) 🔑, B2
status (n.) 🔑 AWL , A1
top (adj.) 🔑, A2

OXFORD
UNIVERSITY PRESS

198 Madison Avenue
New York, NY 10016 USA

Great Clarendon Street, Oxford, OX2 6DP, United Kingdom

Oxford University Press is a department of the University of Oxford.
It furthers the University's objective of excellence in research, scholarship,
and education by publishing worldwide. Oxford is a registered trade
mark of Oxford University Press in the UK and in certain other countries.

First published in 2015

2019 2018 2017 2016 2015

10 9 8 7 6 5 4 3 2 1

Adult Content Director: Stephanie Karras
Publisher: Sharon Sargent
Managing Editor: Mariel DeKranis
Development Editor: Eric Zuarino
Bridget O'Lavin: Head of Digital, Design, and Production
Executive Art and Design Manager: Maj-Britt Hagsted
Design Project Manager: Debbie Lofaso
Content Production Manager: Julie Armstrong
Image Manager: Trisha Masterson
Image Editor: Liaht Ziskind
Production Coordinator: Brad Tucker

ISBN: 978 0 19 482067 7 Student Book 3A with iQ Online pack
ISBN: 978 0 19 482068 4 Student Book 3A as pack component
ISBN: 978 0 19 481802 5 iQ Online student website

Printed in China
This book is printed on paper from certified and well-managed sources.

ACKNOWLEDGEMENTS

*The authors and publisher are grateful to those who have given permission to
reproduce the following extracts and adaptations of copyright material:*

p. 160 from "Happiness Breeds Success ... and Money!" by Sonja
Lyubomirsky, July 18, 2008, http://www.psychologytoday.com. Used by
permission of Sonja Lyubomirsky.

Illustrations by: p. 4 Jing Jing Tsong; p. 28 Bill Smith Group; p. 48 Bill Smith
Group; p. 78 Bill Smith Group; p. 89 Barb Bastian; p. 102 Bill Smith Group;
p. 128 Barb Bastian; p. 152 Barb Bastian; p. 176 Bill Smith Group.

*We would also like to thank the following for permission to reproduce the following
photographs*: Cover: David Pu'u/Corbis; Inside back cover: lvcandy/Getty
Images, Bloom Design/shutterstock; Video Vocabulary (used throughout the
book): Oleksiy Mark / Shutterstock; p. 2/3 MCMULLAN CO/SIPA/Newscom;
p6 Artiga Photo/Corbis UK Ltd.; p. 16 Art Directors & TRIP/Alamy; p. 18
UpperCut/Oxford University Press; p. 26 Ariel Skelley/Blend Images/Cor/
Corbis UK Ltd.; p. 27 Africa Studio/Shutterstock (sweets); p. 27 Wutthichai/
Shutterstock (vitamins); p. 27 Jason Loucas/Getty Images (fest food); p. 30
Jason Loucas/Getty Images; p. 35 Bon Appetit/Alamy (ice cream); p. 35
Steve Cavalier/Alamy (coffee); p. 36 Photodisc/Oxford University Press
(chocolate); p. 36 Photodisc/Oxford University Press (coffee); p. 36 Scott
Karcich/Shutterstock (cheese); p. 41 Stock Connection/Superstock Ltd.; p. 42
Aurelie and Morgan David de Lossy/Getty Images; p. 43 Paul Abbitt/Alamy;
p. 46 luoman/iStockphoto; p. 47 SoFood/Alamy (fondue); p. 47 Tim Hill/
Alamy (paella); p. 48 Stockbyte/Oxford University Press; p. 52/53 Richard
T. Nowitz/Corbis UK Ltd.; p. 56 Tetra Images/Oxford University Press;
p. 61 Rex Features; p. 72 David Madison/Corbis/Oxford University Press;
p. 76 Caro /Alamy; p. 77 SilvaAna/iStockphoto (menu); p. 77 Stacy Walsh
Rosenstock/Alamy (bicycle); p. 78 SeanPavonePhoto/Shutterstock; p. 81
Venus Angel/Shutterstock (pram); p. 81 Timmary/Shutterstock (perfume);
p. 81 Shutterstock/Maksim Kabakou/Oxford University Press (phone);
p. 100/101 Mark Moffett / MINDEN PICTURES/Getty Images; p. 102 Monalyn
Gracia/Corbis UK Ltd.; p. 103 Ariel Skelley/Blend Images/Cor/Corbis UK Ltd.;
p. 111 Stuart Westmorland/Science Fa/Corbis UK Ltd.; p. 122 imagebroker/
Alamy (Pantheon); p. 122 Neus Grandia/Oxford University Press (map);
p. 126 Alistair Berg/Getty Images; p. 126/127 ZING Studio/iStockphoto;
p. 127 Bennyartist/Shutterstock (turbines); p. 127 VLADGRIN /iStockphoto
(illustration); p. 129 HolgerBurmeister/Alamy; p. 134 Moodboard/Corbis
UK Ltd.; p. 137 Subic/Getty Images; p. 140 Huntstock, Inc/Alamy; p. 150/151
Bernd Kohlhas/Corbis UK Ltd.; p. 153 Photodisc/Oxford University Press;
p. 157 Steven S Miric/Superstock Ltd.; p. 159 Simon Jarratt/Corbis UK
Ltd.; p. 160 Dana Patrick/Sonja Lyubomirsky, Ph.D.; p. 165 David Noton
Photography/Alamy; p. 174 Steve Debenport/Getty Images; p. 175 david
pearson/Alamy (medal); p. 175 Marmaduke St. John/Alamy (scoreboard);
p. 176 Photodisc/Oxford University Press (reading); p. 176 Image Source/
Corbis UK Ltd. (runner); p. 176 fStop/Alamy (woman); p. 177 Paul Collis/Alamy;
p. 178 Photodisc/Oxford University Press; p. 180 PCN Photography/Alamy;
p. 182 Moodboard/Corbis UK Ltd.; p. 183 Lebrecht Music and Arts Photo
Library/Alamy.